THE CONFIDENCE SOLUTION

THE CONFIDENCE SOLUTION

Reinvent Your Life, Explode Your Business, Skyrocket Your Income

KEITH JOHNSON

JEREMY P. TARCHER/PENGUIN
a member of Penguin Group (USA) Inc.
New York

JEREMY P. TARCHER/PENGUIN
Published by the Penguin Group
Penguin Group (USA) Inc., 375 Hudson Street, New York, New York 10014, USA • Penguin
Group (Canada), 90 Eglinton Avenue East, Suite 700, Toronto, Ontario M4P 2Y3, Canada
(a division of Pearson Penguin Canada Inc.) • Penguin Books Ltd, 80 Strand, London
WC2R 0RL, England • Penguin Ireland, 25 St Stephen's Green, Dublin 2, Ireland (a division
of Penguin Books Ltd) • Penguin Group (Australia), 250 Camberwell Road, Camberwell,
Victoria 3124, Australia (a division of Pearson Australia Group Pty Ltd) • Penguin Books
India Pvt Ltd, 11 Community Centre, Panchsheel Park, New Delhi–110 017, India • Penguin
Group (NZ), 67 Apollo Drive, Rosedale, North Shore 0632, New Zealand
(a division of Pearson New Zealand Ltd) • Penguin Books (South Africa) (Pty) Ltd,
24 Sturdee Avenue, Rosebank, Johannesburg 2196, South Africa

Penguin Books Ltd, Registered Offices: 80 Strand, London WC2R 0RL, England

Most Tarcher/Penguin books are available at special quantity discounts for bulk purchase for
sales promotions, premiums, fund-raising, and educational needs. Special books or book
excerpts also can be created to fit specific needs. For details, write Penguin Group (USA) Inc.
Special Markets, 375 Hudson Street, New York, NY 10014.

Library of Congress Cataloging-in-Publication Data

Johnson, Keith (Keith E.)
The confidence solution : reinvent your life, explode your business,
skyrocket your income / Keith Johnson.
p.   cm.
ISBN 978-1-58542-865-6
1. Self-confidence.   2. Self-actualization (Psychology).   3. Success.
4. Success in business.   I. Title.
BF575.S39J643   2011   2011003201
158.1—dc22

Printed in the United States of America
1   3   5   7   9   10   8   6   4   2

BOOK DESIGN BY NICOLE LAROCHE

While the author has made every effort to provide accurate telephone numbers and
Internet addresses at the time of publication, neither the publisher nor the author
assumes any responsibility for errors, or for changes that occur after publication.
Further, the publisher does not have any control over and does not assume
any responsibility for author or third-party websites or their content.

I dedicate this book to John P. Kelly. Destiny caused our paths to cross. I was an orphan son who desperately needed a father figure. You saw my potential and knew I needed a caring and loving father who believed in me and what I was doing to spread the message of confidence worldwide. You caused my confidence to take a quantum leap the day you acknowledged, identified, accepted, and affirmed me as your own son.

As I teach in this book, a father's encouragement empowers a son, but a father's criticism cripples a son. Your encouragement empowered me with the greater level of confidence I needed to become more congruent as a leader and to achieve the dream I had of having a book published by Penguin Books.

You are the best father a son could ever ask for. Thank you, Dad, for being in my life!

CONTENTS

CONFIDENCE IS THE SOLUTION!

∾

*Do you feel like you should be much
further along in life by now?*

I speak to thousands of people worldwide, and I ask every crowd this question: *Do you feel like you should be much further along in life by now?* No matter what the culture, political view, economic status, or ethnic background of the group, they respond uniformly: 99 percent admit feeling that they should be accomplishing *much* more in life!

What about you? Are you feeling fearful, uncertain, and doubtful about your future? Do you need a solution or key to unlock the door to your confidence? Are you tired of being stuck in a rut on the road to nowhere? Do you want to eliminate feelings that deny, diminish, and destroy your self-confidence? Are you tired of being surrounded by insecure, unconfident people? Are you overwhelmed by personal or business problems that seem to have no solution?

Who am I to tell you what is true, how to change, and/or how to progress in your life or business? I am a person who has helped thousands from all walks of life to take life-changing steps that moved them forward to fulfill their potential, accomplish their goals, and reach their destiny. The steps thoroughly discussed in this book will do the same for you!

A LIFE-CHANGING DISCOVERY

On March 3, 2002, I dragged myself out of bed after spending another night sleepless due to an incredible amount of financial pressure and personal stress. I went into my office and stared at the stack of unpaid bills on my desk. The feeling of frustration and disappointment weighed down my body, mind, and spirit as I looked at my checkbook's zero balance.

To avoid the pain, I jumped in my car and went to McDonald's to buy breakfast for my wife and me. As I was pulling out of our prestigious gated community in my Cadillac Sedan DeVille, I saw a homeless man beside the road begging for food. *I am only one month away from being in the same condition as this man*, I thought.

I quickly pushed that thought out of my mind and instead tried to think positively about my future. I knew I was destined to be a person of great accomplishments. I had dreams of traveling the world and speaking to millions of people. My dreams included writing a best-selling book that would be distributed worldwide and speaking to multitudes through the media.

Just fifteen minutes later, while I ate a breakfast burrito in our dining room, tears and hysterical sobs overwhelmed me. That day stained my life; it was one of my worst days *ever*. I experienced an emotional, mental, spiritual, and financial breakdown.

*Have you ever felt so low that you
wanted to give up on yourself, family,
God, and even life?*

Everything in and around me imploded. We lost everything! I felt like my life was over. Suicide entered my mind. I looked at my wife and asked, "Why were you so stupid to marry me? You deserve someone so much better. You'll be better off without me."

I repeatedly thought *I am such a loser. I will never amount to anything. There is no way I can recover from this failure. I will never succeed in life. Why does it seem like I take five steps forward only to go ten steps backward? Why do bad things always happen to me?* I had no confidence that day.

During this meltdown I learned the secret of what was stopping me from experiencing outrageous success in life. This secret produced some wonderful results in my life at a rate that was mind-boggling.

Here is what happened to me over the next three short years after discovering this one secret—the solution and key to outrageous success:

- *My income increased.* My income doubled annually.
- *My influence expanded.* I went from never having made a television appearance to appearing on more than thirty-five programs.
- *My joy and happiness skyrocketed.* My spiritual, emotional, and mental health improved.
- *I lost forty pounds.* I got my obesity under control, and started to eat well and exercise regularly.
- *My relationships deepened.* I developed relationships with some of the most respected authorities on leadership development in the world.
- *My possessions multiplied.* In only three years, I was living in the house and driving the car of my dreams.
- *My potential grew exponentially.* I finished and published my book, *The Confidence Makeover,* which reached a global market.

I thought I had a money problem—but the solution to my problem wasn't money. So what was the secret I discovered? What answered the problems overwhelming my life? *The Confidence Solution!*

Successful men and women who also know this to be true include:

- Leadership expert and best-selling author *John Maxwell.* He is continually asked about the greatest qualities a leader must possess. He asserts that the leader's greatest asset is *confidence.* "Confidence in oneself is the cornerstone of leadership. It is difficult for those who do not believe in themselves to have much faith in anyone else. **Self-confidence brings confidence in others.**"[1]

❧ *Meg Whitman*, who in seven years grew eBay from zero to 50 million customers and into a multi-billion-dollar global corporation. Before stepping down as CEO to run for governor of California, she said of her leadership priorities, "Hire the right person for the right job at the right time and who has the right values. I cannot stress this enough. Reorganize early and often. **Transform change and uncertainty into opportunity.**"[2]

❧ *Darren Hardy, Success* magazine publisher and editorial director, said, "Whether leading a nation, a multi-billion-dollar corporation, a small sales team, or a family, the qualities of a leader are the same. **A leader instills confidence and helps people become more than they are.** Leaders illuminate the path for others to journey forward, farther than they thought possible by themselves."

❧ Who can argue the business wisdom of the man who founded the dominant retail chain in the United States—Wal-Mart. *Sam Walton* said, "Outstanding leaders go out of their way to boost the self-esteem of their personnel. **If**

1 John Maxwell, *Success* magazine, February 2010, p. 18.

2 The article titled "Innovation and Leadership Lessons from Meg Whitman, eBay CEO and President, and Top Innovator" can be found at the following website: http://creativityandinnovation.blogspot.com/2007/05/innovation-and-leadership-from.html.

people believe in themselves, it's amazing what they can accomplish."

So what is *confidence*?

Confidence is a positive belief in yourself, your potential, and your abilities. Confidence produces a feeling of certainty and hope empowering you to perform at your best, create workable solutions to your problems, think big about your future, take calculated risks, and act effectively to achieve extraordinary, outrageous results, and success for you and others.

The solution I discovered to dispel my fears, uncertainties, and doubts in life was *confidence*. If your confidence is in the tank, you desperately need to learn the secrets revealed in this book now!

Or you may be thinking, *I have lots of confidence, at times too much, but those around me don't have enough.* Not only does *your* confidence need to grow, but you also need the skill and power to impart and instill confidence in others. This book isn't only about building up *your* confidence; it also discusses in detail how you can empower those around you with the Confidence Solution. Everyone can learn from this book as well: family members, colleagues at work, people in your church or synagogue, friends, and associates.

The following is an overview of what you will be discovering beginning with the Confidence Solution for Success. This triangle contains many smaller triangles. I designed this to be used like a bookshelf that you can go to when you are facing different problems or need empowerment in certain areas of your personal and professional life. Look it over. I will cover each of these triangles throughout your reading of *The Confidence Solution.*

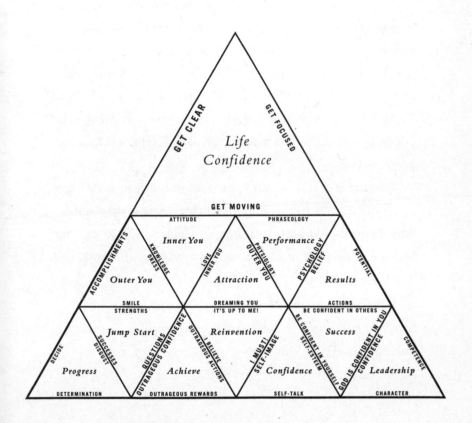

Triangles help you remember and visualize steps to take to move out of fear, uncertainty, and doubt into a particular transformational process that will help you build your Confidence Solution.

Why a triangle? A triangle is balanced, connected, and simple. All the steps influence and affect one another as you make progress. Each point on the triangle represents a step toward reinventing yourself, exploding your business, and skyrocketing your income.

The triangle shape is frequently used in construction for strength, durability, and the ability to handle pressure on each side. Triangles are used in the trusses in the international space station, the ancient pyramids of Egypt, and on the strongest bridge design, known in architecture as the truss bridge. These triangles will inform and instruct you on how to take your Confidence Solution to the peak and experience outrageous success.

Starting today, you can *confidently* join me in creating a successful and fulfilling life! Even though you may not be where you should be or want to be right now, you can get back on track and quickly accelerate toward your destiny.

Confidence Level Assessment

HOW CONFIDENT ARE YOU?

Answer the following questions to begin your journey of self-discovery! This self-assessment will allow you to measure where you see yourself with regard to your current level of self-confidence.

Rate yourself on a scale of 0–10 according to how much you believe each of the following statements to be true.

0 = you think the statement is totally false.

10 = you think the statement is completely true.

_____ 1. I love myself as a person.

_____ 2. I really believe in myself.

_____ 3. I am as good as everyone else.

_____ 4. I feel like I am very successful.

_____ 5. I know I am very smart.

_____ 6. When I look into the mirror, I like everything I see.

_____ 7. I am worth millions of dollars.

_____ 8. I don't feel like a failure.

_____ 9. I love and embrace change.

_____ 10. I have a positive outlook on life.

_____ 11. I don't want to be like anybody else.

_____ 12. I am not afraid to ask for what I want.

_____ 13. What others say or do to me has no effect on me.

_____ 14. I love talking to others.

_____ 15. I have the ability to make myself a success.

_____ 16. I am an expert in my field.

_____ 17. I love to take a risk.

_____ 18. I am not afraid to make mistakes.

_____ 19. I can laugh at myself.

_____ 20. I have written goals and plans for my future.

Total Score: _____

ASSESSMENT RESULTS

170–200 You have a high level of self-confidence. You do need to fine-tune and increase your confidence in a couple of key areas, though. Improve these areas and you'll be ready to be a confidence coach to others.

135–169 You have a medium to high ranking in your level of self-confidence. Sometimes you are a confident person. However, there are times when your confidence can be totally bankrupt. You need to learn how to maintain high levels of confidence on a consistent basis. You need to fine-tune and increase your confidence in several different areas. A life coach will give you the encouragement you need to maintain a high level of confidence.

100–134 You have very low levels of self-confidence. You lack confidence in yourself in most areas. You need a daily confidence-building plan and a life coach.

0–99 Your confidence is as low as it can get. Your emotional state is at serious risk. The smartest decision you ever made was to start reading this book. You can change your life. Visit our website and invest in some of our confidence-boosting material. Get a life coach. It's time for a Confidence Makeover. You should not try to complete this challenge alone!

ADDITIONAL SUPPORT

The Confidence Assessment Test™ is a new revolutionary system designed to help you discover specific problem areas where you personally lack confidence. For an in-depth assessment report, go to www.ConfidenceSolution.com or contact our office.

Chapter 1

ACCELERATE YOUR CONFIDENCE

∞

IN the present season of economic challenges, the confidence of many people is plummeting. Successful professionals and day laborers alike have experienced cuts, layoffs, and terminations.

Talk about a blow to self-confidence! Losing your equity and home in addition to losing your job, retirement, and health insurance is certain to cause emotional and mental turmoil. Unemployment nationwide hovered around 10 percent for months during 2008 and early 2009. Unemployment has doubled since December 2007 with more than 231,000 people losing their jobs in just Florida alone! The world economy has endured the worst recession in fifty years.

The Defining Moment

As I wrote earlier, my depression and loss of confidence left me feeling defeated and depressed. While my faith in God kept me from suicide, I can certainly understand the devastating effects caused by loss of confidence. What pushed me toward life instead of depression and death?

When my confidence was shattered, what secret, what hidden reality, was revealed while I felt so utterly defeated that day? I had a defining moment—a moment that radically changed me. Many people think it takes a long time to reinvent your life. If you believe it takes a long time, you will never have the drive to turn who you are into something better. Reinventing yourself or your organization does not take a long time; it just takes a long time to get to the moment where you are so totally disgusted with your circumstances that you are willing to change.

Get Disgusted!

Disgust is one of the most powerful emotions a human being can have. When you say, "I've had it! I'm tired of this! I can't take it anymore! I must do something about me or my business now!" you are positioning yourself for a positive, real-life breakthrough, conversion, and turnaround. Being in a state of absolute disgust is a perfect place for transformation.

- Is your life or business at a standstill?
- Are you tired of just getting by?
- Are you ready to let go of the pain?

❦ Are you ready to eliminate the hindrances and let go of the restraints?

After my pity party that morning, I started thinking about my past "learning experiences" (also known as "failures and mistakes"), and I realized that I had to get the FUD out of my life! FUD = Fear, Uncertainty, and Doubt. What is the cure for the FUD disease that infects people? THE POWER OF CONFIDENCE!

CONFIDENCE COACHING SOLUTION
Progress demands confronting fear.

That day I discovered an awesome reality: My own FUD were hindering me from obtaining the success in life I desired. In one defining moment, I made a life-changing decision: *I was going to overcome these restraints and build up my confidence to an all-time high.* I would intensely pursue the subject of *confidence.* What is it? Where does it come from? How can I build it? When do I need it? How will it help me in life? How can I harness its power to help me change and progress toward my destiny? The commitment I made then has not only helped me build my confidence, but it has also helped countless people do the same.

Over the past ten years I have been consumed with finding the answers to these four questions:

1. What is the difference between those who succeed and those who fail?
2. What is the key difference between peak performers, those who are at the top of their game, and average performers?
3. What is the fastest way to improve a person's life so he or she can reach desired results?
4. What hinders or distracts people from changing and making progress?

As I found the answers to these questions, I cranked up and accelerated my confidence beyond what I had even hoped for. My faith in God bolstered my confidence, and I remembered this promise: "So do not throw away your confidence; it will be richly rewarded."[1]

So I sought answers that would restore and strengthen my confidence, and bring reward and blessing into my life and the lives of others. You will find the answers to these questions in the following chapters, and as you remove the FUD (fears, uncertainty, doubt) from your life, you will accelerate your confidence too!

Accelerate Your Confidence

"Drivers, start your engines!" A stock car, dragster, or high-performance car has great potential. However, until the en-

---

1 Hebrews 10:35 (NIV).

gine starts, the car cannot operate at its full potential. The horsepower of the engine determines the car's top speed and how quickly it can accelerate from a dead stop.

Confidence is the fuel that empowers you to maximize your performance, potential, and profits. Most people's internal engines are totally shut down. Just like a race car, the only way to achieve extraordinary performance is to start the engine.

Every person is born with an internal engine designed to run on the fuel of confidence. Our childhood environment, the models exemplified before us, and the words that were spoken to us have either disabled our engines with negativity or fueled us with confidence.

When I was seventeen years of age, my grandpa helped me buy a 1969 Ford Galaxie convertible with a 390 engine. I loved to jump into that car, start the engine, slam down the accelerator, and peel out in a cloud of smoke and burning rubber. After about a year of driving the car, I noticed the engine was not performing very well. Black smoke was coming out of the rear muffler. The car didn't peel out when I floored the accelerator; it poked along.

"Do you know what is wrong with my car?" I asked Dad.

"When was the last time you changed the oil?" he replied.

"Oil? I didn't know I had to do that."

The next day I took my Galaxie to the shop to get an oil change. I watched as the mechanic removed the drain plug and drained the oil that was black and very thick with dirt. After a fresh drink of oil, my car was back in operation. Of course

I had to test it by slamming down the accelerator—yep, she was back to normal performance.

Unless protected and maintained regularly, your internal confidence engine tends to attract FUD that limit your life, business, and financial potential. Like a highly certified precision mechanic, I will help you identify and eliminate the FUD inside your engine so you can accelerate toward your destiny, unleash your potential, and explode your income.

Four Internal Engine Conditions

I've discovered that there are four actions needed to restore your confidence to peak performance. You may need to:

1. **Overhaul Your Engine**—Your confidence is at an all-time low and you need a total life makeover. This may be easier than you think. I will help you through each step toward transforming your life into one you are excited to live!

2. **Change the Oil**—Oil flows through the engine collecting dirt. For the engine to perform at maximum potential, you must change the oil. Sometimes the negative forces of our culture can cause the dirt of fear, uncertainty, and doubt to clog your engine and limit your potential.

3. **Have a Tune-up**—If you have a six-cylinder engine with just one bad spark plug, your engine will not perform at its best. The same is true of your life or business; you can

be confident in financial achievements, but unhappy in your relationships. A tune-up will revive your relationship cylinder, which may need a new spark plug to fine-tune your success.

4. **Install a Turbo**—You may be a highly confident, successful, and well-balanced person. However, your current horsepower can be supercharged with a turbo so you can go from success to significance, from a dream to leaving a lasting legacy. Or you may be the mechanic who helps others make an oil change or install a turbo—instilling confidence in those who need it.

Continuing with my automotive analogy, you may find yourself associating with the following types of people:

- **Super-chargers**—These are people who have more confidence and success than you have. They know how to accelerate confidence and move out of the pits. They can help you achieve your goals. They have already achieved success and will not be intimidated or jealous because you want the same result.
- **Starters**—Positive people who are presently in your life who support you and cause your engine to start when you are around them.
- **Parachutes**—These are negative people who drag you down and hold you back. These are people from your past who "remember who you used to be" and want you to stay

that way. These people are hard to remove from your life, but to move forward you must cut the Parachutes' cords or they will hold you back from accelerating toward your destiny.

You have to cut your ties with Parachutes if you want to be empowered by the Super-chargers and Starters in life. Super-chargers and Starters fuel your confidence; hang around them. Parachutes are filled with FUD; cut them loose. Embrace people with positive, confident attitudes.

Remember, "The greatest revolution of our generation is the discovery that human beings, by changing the inner attitudes of their minds, can change the outer aspects of their lives."[2]

No Excuses, Just Results

Ask any of my family members, any of our team members, or any of my clients, "What is Keith's favorite saying?" You will hear the same answer from everyone, every time: "No excuses, just results!"

I am an "all things are possible" guy. I believe in positive thinking and talking. I believe much of that positive thinking comes from God. I feel loved by my Creator and believe that God has good plans for me. In fact, He says, "For I know the

---

2 Jack Canfield, *The Success Principles: How to Get from Where You Are to Where You Want to Be* (New York: Harper Paperbacks, 2006), p. 187.

plans I have for you. . . . They are plans for good and not for disaster, to give you a future and a hope."[3] But that potential from the Creator must be acted upon. Positive, confident thinking must produce positive actions. At the end of the day, I want to see the results of what you say you believe and think. I don't offer people the opportunity to become a member of my team based on their potential. I invite them because of the *results* they have already produced.

Many people step up to my book-signing table after a keynote presentation and declare, "I want to buy your Confidence Coaching System and your Confidence Makeover book for my _____ [husband, wife, son, daughter, grandchildren, salespeople, leaders, etc.]. They desperately need it."

My response is often "What about you?"

"Oh, I'm doing fine," they reply.

Many times, though, it is obvious from their nonverbal communication—physiology, dress, weight, body language, tone of voice, and facial expression—that they are actually screaming "I LACK CONFIDENCE!"

Building Confidence Requires the Power of Change

Positive change is the process of inventing or reinventing a person or organization to fulfill destiny. Most people and organizations trap themselves in one identity and never change,

3 Jeremiah 29:11 (NLT).

modify, or update who they have become (identity) over the years due to life experiences, and they haven't considered who they will become in the future.

I invite you to see your life from a fresh perspective that will help you convert past paradigms and thoughts to new, confident thoughts that will empower your progress toward prosperity.

Nothing extraordinary has ever been achieved *except* by those who dared to have the confidence to believe that something inside of them was superior to outward circumstances. Changing from FUD to confidence requires overcoming perceived limitations. Henry Winkler, the quintessential, always upbeat Fonzie from the American television sitcom *Happy Days* had FUD times in life. He also has words of wisdom on confidently overcoming problems and affirming the need for confidence: "When I was growing up, it took me a long, long time to find my confidence. When you have a learning challenge and you're not keeping up, it works on your self-image. I think the beginning and the end of living is keeping your self-image intact and strong, and as a parent, keeping your child's self-image strong. Because when that goes, almost everything goes."[4]

Deep inside each of us is an inner hunger for something more—something deeper, richer, and lasting. Each of us has

4 Marie Speed, "Your Personal Best: Henry Winkler," *Success,* http://www.success magazine.com/your-personal-best-henry-winkler/PARAMS/article/797.

some inner uncertainty that, no matter how great our lives already are, there is yet another level—one of passion, gratitude, connection, justice, righteousness, joy, happiness, and success.

So the big question isn't "Do I have a problem?"

Instead, it is "Do I have the same problem I had last year?"

Dr. Phil's big question when people are stuck in the same old cycles of failure: "How has that been working for you?"

Your personal and organizational *history* is a snapshot of your *future*—unless you change the present. You cannot change what you tolerate. If you tolerate a $30,000-a-year income, you will never reach for $100,000 a year. If you tolerate earning $100,000 a year, you will not make the necessary changes to produce $1 million a year. If you tolerate underachievers working as business employees, you will never fire them so you can get higher-quality people to take your company to the next level. Likewise, if you tolerate your spouse treating you badly, he or she will not know how to treat you with respect.

The Battle for Results

Life involves warfare. You must win the *internal* battles before you will see the *external* results you really want in your life or business. Your external life is merely a result of how well you are doing at winning the internal warfare.

Consider these points:

- Your yearly income is an external result.
- Your weight is an external result.
- Your health is an external result.
- Your achievements are an external result.
- Your business profits are an external result.
- Your portfolio is an external result.
- Your relationships are an external result.
- Your enthusiasm for life is an external result.

You may think you are confident, but what are your results revealing? Are you truly happy with your outcomes?

Most people today do not like the external results they are producing in life so they try to change the *external*. They don't like certain aspects of their lives so they change jobs, geographical locations, churches, schools, cars, and even their physical appearance. Today, if you don't like your life, you can easily change spouses, your hair color, your name, your nose, and so on. Everybody is consumed with changing the external, not realizing that every time you make a change, you keep taking "you" with you. Yes! You continue to carry the baggage of your problem along with the thinking that something or someone else is the problem. The problem is *internal*. Change does not happen externally; it must start internally. Change must also be accompanied by the desire and intention to strategically plan and implement how you will progress from now into your future destiny.

Most people are working hard to change, but they don't see the results they want and deserve.

Do you sometimes feel like a world-class sprinter who is stuck in a mud puddle? Running hard? Busy? But not making any progress? I once felt that way. But after my defining moment, I realized that I could increase and accelerate my confidence as I looked under the hood into the internal engine of myself.

The Confidence Index

So how can you measure change, progress, and increasing confidence? With the Confidence Index! In these trying financial times, we often hear about the *Consumer Confidence Index*—a measure of consumer optimism about current economic conditions. Economists often consider consumer *confidence* to be an important indicator of the future health of a nation's economy. Likewise, a *Personal Confidence Index* can be an important indicator of your future physical, emotional, relational, and financial health.

Although people are writing and talking about the importance of confidence, my challenge was "How do I measure a person's level of confidence?" After much research and hundreds of hours of consulting and interviewing, I created *The Confidence Thermostat.*

The Confidence Thermostat

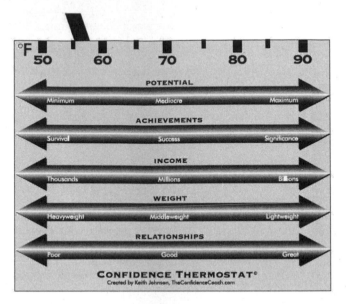

CONFIDENCE THERMOSTAT©
Created by Keith Johnson, TheConfidenceCoach.com

*Confidence is the thermostat that regulates
your degree of success in life.*

If you think that you have been taking five steps forward but ten steps backward, your thermostat may be dictating that frustrating process. Every person has what I call an *internal Confidence Thermostat setting*. This setting regulates the degree of results a person actually produces in life. A thermostat is designed to turn on the furnace when the room temperature goes lower than its setting. So when you start going backward and your confidence temperature falls below your normal thermostat setting, you feel motivated to do all the things you have learned in the past to regain your confidence.

Those old tried-and-true self-motivational attitudes or actions may or may not help. If you have to struggle too long or it's too hard, you may simply lower your thermostat setting and lose even more confidence in yourself.

Likewise, when your confidence takes a leap forward due to a success or victory in life, you may ride the tide of that income increase, relationship improvement, momentary victory, or loss of weight; and then as time passes, the excitement of the moment wanes and your thermostat setting pulls you back into your comfort zone. Instead of setting your thermostat higher and changing your attitudes and behavior to adjust to more confidence in your life, you simply ease back to where you were. The old saying "A dog will return to its vomit" is so true. Confidence gained through the "thrill of victory" becomes a memory instead of a lifestyle and thermostat change for the better. Rather than raising all of your attitudes and actions to a higher confidence level, you safely retreat to "what's been" instead of living in the newness of "what can be."

I believe that the majority of people around us are underachievers. They are not unleashing their full potential. Their thermostats are set at 55 degrees. Just imagine what could happen to a company's sales force if every salesperson increased his or her thermostat setting by just 20 degrees. Cash flow would instantly multiply. Excitement, energy, and morale would return to the sales force and the bottom line would increase. What is possible if the entire company increased its Confidence Thermostat? An explosion in the business. I have seen it work over and over again. Let's look more closely at the five indicators on *The Confidence Thermostat*.

1. POTENTIAL: MINIMUM—MEDIOCRE—MAXIMUM

Examine your current life conditions compared to what you know you are capable of achieving. *Potential is who you can become, what more you can achieve, what more you can have, who else you can help.*

2. ACHIEVEMENTS: SURVIVAL—SUCCESS—SIGNIFICANCE

Examine your life according to what you have actually achieved so far. Are you living in survival mode? Do you have *just enough* to pay your bills? What would happen to your finances if you were unemployed for one month and received no pay?

Maybe you are you in the success mode. Have you obtained success in the eyes of your peers, family, and others? Do others look up to you? Do you have the ability to help others who need it?

Have you grown beyond the desire for success—are you now reaching for significance, the ability to leave a positive, lasting legacy long after death? Have you generated enough wealth to see to it that your organization will continue to help solve problems and meet needs in the world one hundred years after your death?

3. INCOME: THOUSANDS—MILLIONS—BILLIONS

I like this gauge because it is measurable. All we have to do is examine your portfolio. What is your income? How much money and how many assets do you have? Thousands? Millions? Billions? What are you saving, investing, and giving?

4. WEIGHT: HEAVYWEIGHT—MIDDLEWEIGHT—LIGHTWEIGHT

Examine your weight. According to the ideal medical weight for your height and body structure, are you a lightweight, middleweight, or a heavyweight? If weight control has been a continual struggle for you, don't despair. When you fine-tune your internal engine, your confidence will be accelerated, and you will soon find yourself in optimal shape.

5. RELATIONSHIPS: POOR—GOOD—GREAT

Examine your relationships. Start with your family or friends. Are those relationships poor, good, or great? How about the people you spend the most time with? Poor relationships consist of those people who accept you the way you are, or were. An example of a poor relationship is when you frequently argue with your spouse, don't enjoy each other's company, and have a hard time communicating. Good relationships are ones with people who are equal to you in goals and attitudes;

you sharpen each other. Great relationships are ones with people who are where you want to be and their relationship changes you for the better.

What are the initial *results* from reviewing your Personal Confidence Index? Cool? Warm? Hot? Not where they need to be? Are you experiencing outcomes other than what you really want? Most people believe that they can produce results if everything goes perfectly.

CONFIDENCE COACHING SOLUTION
Confidence rises in producing results
regardless of circumstances.

DECIDE TO BE UNCOMFORTABLE

Thermostats are all about making the environment comfortable. To experience progress you must get comfortable with being uncomfortable. Do you really want to experience outrageous success, or do you want to be comfortable? Most people are comfortable, and this is a huge problem if they want to realize success. Most people do not really want to make the adjustments necessary to reinvent their lives, explode their businesses, and skyrocket their incomes. When you are comfortable, you don't feel too hot or too cold.

But when the temperature in your room makes you uncomfortable, it breeds a desire to make a new adjustment in your thermostat. You have to be uncomfortable to want to make changes in your life. Increase the setting on your Confidence Thermostat! As a confidence coach, my job is to stretch and push you to make a "no-turning-back decision" to go beyond what is comfortable for you. A rubber band does not fulfill its potential until it is stretched—and neither do you.

The decision is yours. Do you really want to experience outrageous success?

Whatever temperature your Confidence Thermostat is set on, you will naturally attract people and opportunities that are comfortable for you. For instance, if a single person's thermostat is set at 50 degrees, he or she will be drawn to develop a relationship with another person whose income is under $100,000. This person will not attract someone whose income is in the millions. Why? The internal thermostat is set for thousands, not millions or billions. This single person will attract a person who is also living life in survival mode, who is not performing at his or her full potential, and is probably not in good health.

> *In no other field of endeavor does self-confidence or the lack of it play such an important part as in the field of salesmanship.*
>
> —Napoleon Hill, author of *Think and Grow Rich*

What about the mediocre salespeople? Most salespeople's thermostats are set at 60 degrees. They consistently make between $60,000 and $80,000 every year. Why? Because that is where their thermostats are set. I have seen some salespeople reach their yearly goals by the third quarter and then they totally bomb out the rest of the year with practically no sales. The majority of salespeople never break past the $100,000-$250,000-, or $1 million-a-year mark.

The 55-degree person settles for a mediocre life. Let me ask you, "Do dogs like bones?" Most people answer YES! The answer is NO! They like meat. However, they "settle" for the bones. Most people settle for too little in life. Many are stuck where they are because they have had so many bones; all they think about is bones. It never crosses their minds that they do not have to settle, that they can have the meat. Mark Twain quipped, "Human beings are like dust; they tend to settle."

Consider the financial indicator on your thermostat for a moment. Would Donald Trump ever be satisfied with $1 million in the bank? Where is his financial thermostat set? Billions. What about you? What is your comfort zone? I know people who, whenever they receive large chunks of money, always end up broke again. They say things like "I don't know what I'd do if I had no debt." "I just don't care about money. It's not important to me." That is why they don't have any of it! Whatever is important to you, you will value and care for it.

What about the weight indicator? When I think of fitness gurus, I think of martial arts trainer and actor Billy Blanks, creator of the Tae Bo exercise program. Would he be satisfied with being twenty pounds overweight? Where is Billy's fitness thermostat set? Lightweight. One of my friends is always dieting, but always overweight. He knows all the solutions to losing weight, but after a season of trying a program involving fitness, nutrition, and discipline, he gravitates back to his comfort zone of being pleasingly plump.

DISGUSTED? THEN WHAT'S NEXT?

Consider the Progress Triangle, which can help you accelerate your confidence and empower your progress.

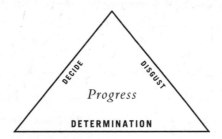

Earlier I emphasized that until we become thoroughly disgusted with ourselves and our decisions, we will not change. Disgust is just the first step to transformation. I use a triangle to explain how to move from disgust to positive action.

Look at the triangle above.

Disgust. When an aspect of your life, business performance, attitude, or actions disgusts you, you have reached an awareness of a particular problem that is pulling you down instead of moving you up.

Decide. Then you must choose to do something rather than remain stuck in disgust.

CONFIDENCE COACHING SOLUTION

It is your decisions—not your conditions—
that shape the future outcome of your life.

If you choose not to change and progress, then you have already made a decision, haven't you?

There are "3 Ds to Quick Start Your Progress" as you decide to change: *decide to lift* your personal expectations; *decide to destroy* limiting belief systems; and *decide to develop* a change strategy.

1. *Decide to lift your personal expectations*—You must choose to raise your own personal standard in every area of your life: confidence levels, weight, potential, income, happiness, and so on. The most important decision I made in reinventing myself was to increase the standard of what I demanded of myself. My life started to change the moment I realized that *my life was not shaped by my conditions, but by my decisions.* I decided who I wanted to be, do, have, and help in my life. I also decided what I would no longer tolerate in my life. If you think about it, many times your standards may drop because you keep company with people who have lower standards. Your life will be defined by the expectations of the people with whom you surround yourself. The old adages apply: "If you lie down with dogs, you will get up with fleas. . . . Birds of a feather flock

together." Say to yourself, *I must keep my personal standards high and not allow others to pull me down.*

2. *Decide to destroy limiting belief systems*—If you raise your personal expectations but do not really believe change is possible, you will sabotage yourself. It's not what you need to "learn" that will make you experience outrageous success in life, but what you need to "unlearn" that is actually more important. You must identify what wrong belief systems you learned in the past that are keeping you from becoming who you are destined to be. Elevating your confidence to a higher level will empower you to achieve the new standards you have set for yourself before you start activating your new change strategy.

3. *Decide to develop a change strategy*—The ability to navigate from where you are to where you want to be requires a map. Being positive is not enough. It doesn't matter how positive you are, if you run east looking for a sunset, you simply will not find it! You need the right strategy. How do you find it? Success leaves clues! When you do the same things and think the same way, you get the same results. Take as much time to plan a step-by-step action plan for your reinvention as you would to map out a two-week vacation.

Determination. The decision to change requires determination to persist and to persevere through to a solution or resolution, moving you beyond disgust to a higher degree of confidence.

CONFIDENCE COACHING SOLUTION

Be determined to embrace the
power of progress.

Progress is the passionate pursuit of your own personal and professional improvement. The success of your personal or organizational future lies in your ability to continually reinvent yourself. The price of progress is change. Happiness, excitement, and fulfillment come from your continual pursuit of progress. Progress shows up in the form of change, growth, and contribution.

Your ability to continually improve yourself is also the key to staying relevant. Most people and organizations fail to improve themselves constantly and therefore become extinct. If you and your organization remain the same while culture, technology, media, and fashion continue to change at an accelerated rate, you will be left behind and deserted.

As long as you stay in your comfort zone and resist change, you will be trapped by *sameness*. Sameness is the ball and chain that limits you and robs you of reaching your maximum potential in life. Change and progress require you to let go of the old and seize new attitudes, new actions, and, most important, new determination. To have a different result, you must be determined to consistently do things differently. If you have not yet gained the wealth, the health, the whole relation-ships, the freedom, or the success you deserve, you must embrace change that initiates progress.

As you continue reading and begin to take the recommended confidence-building steps, you will walk through a process of constructive change that has worked successfully for thousands.

CONFIDENCE COACHING SOLUTION

Change that initiates progress does not take a long time. You can quickly change your life for the better!

In order for your life to change and make progress, *you* must change. For your life to get better, first *you* must get better. If you don't change in your present, the same failures will follow you into your future. Without making some radical changes, your past will be a snapshot of your future outcomes.

Possibility-Thinking Affirmations

To embrace the possibility of change, you can encourage yourself with the testimony of others. The first affirmation: Use the Testimony of Others. Adopt the attitude, "If you can do it, I can do it!"

The following is a testimony sent to me by a CEO who walked through my Confidence Makeover program:

As a young child and an adult, I have always felt inadequate regardless of what I was doing, allowing fear and negative thoughts to control my life. This made my wife, kids, and the employees of our business feel this same exact way. When I began to study the confidence coaching system by Keith Johnson, it was like God turned a light on in my head. I now know I am responsible for controlling my thoughts and that is the key to great action.

This is not something that takes months and years to do; after just a few weeks I am the most confident person I know. My wife, daughter, and I have started working out, eating right, and losing weight. This is so infectious I have purchased over thirty copies of the Confidence Makeover *book and gave them to my sales consultants, managers, and family. I am amazed at the change it has made in everyone and business as a whole—everyone enjoys coming to work, and the company sales have shot up dramatically.*

My relationship with my wife has changed to the point that I think we are falling in love all over again. I am now convinced that lack of confidence is not just a problem in this world, it is an epidemic.

Thank you,
Jim Sipes, CEO

Nebraska Seamless Inc.

The second affirmation: Use Your Own Testimony. Adopt the attitude, "If I did it before, I can do it again!" Keep a journal of what you are thinking and doing to change. After weeks and months pass, you can read what you have written and remember the trials and the triumphs, great and small, that you experienced. Those memories, when summarized, will become your personal testimony and you will see your Confidence Index rising!

We must *change the thermostat* on our Confidence Index. We can analyze all day where our Confidence Thermostat is and why it's there. But the truth is, increasing confidence requires change—turning up the heat!

Confidence is not everything, but it is the one thing that can make a HUGE difference in your personal and professional life. Confidence is an inward root that is manifested externally by the fruit it produces.

If I Were More Confident . . .

We began this journey asking, *Shouldn't I be further along in life by now?* If you answered *yes*, then you read on and discovered that the secret ingredient is confidence, which is needed to move forward and upward to increase the quality of your life. So what if there is a practical, real, and doable way to start over again and create the life you want and deserve? Would you be interested in learning how?

If we are really honest with ourselves, most of us would be excited for an opportunity to start all over again.

CONFIDENCE COACHING SOLUTION

Get excited and enthusiastic about your opportunity to start over, change, progress, and accelerate your confidence.

If you were more confident, how would your life be different?

Would you:

* Already have that pay raise you've earned?
* Have more friends?
* Be reaching the top of your career ladder?
* Be married to the person you've been dating?
* Own the home of your dreams?
* Have started the business you've thought about?
* Be happier and more content?

Yes. Yes. Yes. Yes. Yes. Yes. Yes. The answer is YES!

CONFIDENCE COACHING SOLUTION

A casual attitude about change, progress, and success will lead you toward a life of bitter disappointment and utter frustration.

You may decide to lose weight, stop smoking, start a new business, become debt free, exercise every day, or whatever. During a small window of time, you experience a sudden surge of confidence! "I can do this! I can change my life!" The surge of confidence gives you the ability to make positive changes in your life.

However, that small window of time closes all too soon. Why?

On your journey to reaching your goal, you can run into some obstacles to your *progress*. In a moment of intense pressure or during a time of discouragement, you may *regress* to old patterns and eat that piece of chocolate cake, smoke that cigarette, skip going to the gym, or buy that flat-screen television.

These obstacles can cause you to lose the confident, "I can do this" attitude, and so you return to your old ho-hum pattern of living.

After years of trying to make your life better with no apparent results and waning commitment, you may have developed habits of quitting and doubting yourself rather than habits of success and confidence.

Life isn't easy, and going it alone is even harder. You need a mentor, a confidence coach, a daily voice in your ear saying "YOU CAN DO IT!" If you are longing to be all that you are destined to be, now is the time for you to reinvent yourself and accelerate your confidence.

- *Imagine* what you could accomplish if every day someone came alongside and helped you move toward your dreams.

- *Envision* how you would feel if someone reminded you of how incredible you are—pointing out your strengths and talents.

- *Change and make progress* toward your destiny. You can accelerate your confidence now!

- *Dream* what would be yours if you lived life with confidence.

- *Imagine, envision, change, initiate progress, dream—and live it!*

In the following chapters, I come alongside you to give you the tools and practical applications to move you quickly toward personal and professional greatness. Turn up the thermostat—read on and accelerate your confidence!

America's Confidence Coach Reminds You . . .

- Progress demands confronting fear.
- Confidence is the thermostat that regulates your degree of success in life.
- It is your decisions, not your conditions, that shape the future outcome of your life.
- Change that initiates progress does not take a long time. You can quickly change your life for the better!

- Get excited and enthusiastic about your opportunity to start over, change, progress, and accelerate your confidence.
- A casual attitude about change, progress, and success will lead you toward a life of bitter disappointment and utter frustration.

CONFIDENCE MAKEOVER STEPS NOW!

1. Discover where your Confidence Thermostat is set.

Below is each Confidence Index. Write on the line below it what you feel the current temperature setting is in your life. Refer to page 26 and 27 for an accurate evaluation.

POTENTIAL

0° Minimum	50° Mediocre	100° Maximum

ACHIEVEMENTS

0° Survival	50° Success	100° Significance

INCOME

0° Thousands	50° Millions	100° Billions

WEIGHT

0° Heavyweight	50° Middleweight	100° Lightweight

RELATIONSHIPS

0° Poor	50° Good	100° Great

Now add together the five temperature numbers you have written and then divide the sum by five. Your thermostat setting is _____.

2. At the end of the next twelve months, where would you like your Confidence Thermostat to be set for each index? Write a second number on each index line. Add those five numbers together and divide the total by five. Your new Confidence Thermostat setting goal is _____.

3. Check the steps you are willing to take to begin moving toward your new thermostat setting.

☐ I know that I can change.

☐ I choose to reset the thermostat setting for my weight.

☐ I have decided to reset my thermostat setting for my potential.

☐ I choose to reset my thermostat setting for my income.

☐ I have decided to reset my thermostat setting for my achievements.

☐ I will connect with people around me whose Confidence Thermostat is set higher than mine.

☐ I will read this entire book.

☐ I will empower all of my employees or colleagues at work with confidence-building material.

Chapter 2

THE CRISIS OF CONFIDENCE

∞

WERE you always so confident? That's the number one question people ask me during television interviews, during question-and-answer time at seminars, and while I am autographing books. The answer is a big "NO!" As a matter of fact, I remember at age twenty feeling so insecure and fearful that after receiving an overcharge of $400 from the telephone company, instead of phoning the company and bringing this to their attention, I just paid the bill. Having gone from being afraid to talk on the phone to being a professional speaker, I am now doing the number one thing most feared and hated by so many people. As a matter of fact, some people fear speaking in public more than dying.

I know firsthand what it is like to hit rock bottom with self-doubt and lack of confidence. I have created confidence-building strategies because I felt the pain of failure, fear, and self-doubt, and wanted to rise above my problems and become successful. My bumpy road to becoming America's Confidence Coach began when I flunked kindergarten. Yes! I actually failed kindergarten. I am still puzzled today by the thought *How did I flunk coloring?*

I can still replay that event in my life like it was yesterday. While all my other classmates were having a last-day celebration party, my kindergarten teacher called my mother and me into her office. She told us that I was a slow learner. What I heard that day was that I was dumb and stupid. Believing what I was told greatly hindered my ability to read and write. I was able to make it to the fifth grade by leveraging the one thing I did have—charisma. I became friends with all the really smart girls, and I had an amazing ability to telescope my eyes from my test paper to their test papers.

However, my fifth-grade teacher found out that I could barely read or write. I was called into her office and she told me the same words my kindergarten teacher spoke to me: "You are a slow learner. You should be reading and writing at a much higher level by now. I must hold you back for another year." Again I felt the pain of being left out, being a failure, and believing I was stupid.

However, I leveraged the one strength that has really pushed me to where I am now—my desire to succeed. I begged my teacher to find me a tutor, and I promised to do my best. Thankfully, my reading and writing skills increased enough that the teacher let me go on to sixth grade. Sadly, though, I cheated most of my way through high school and received my diploma. Yes—the Confidence Coach cheated his way through school, and by age twenty-two, I had not read an entire book.

Realizing that my lack of confidence had to be overcome, I set in place key principles that brought me business success and helped me earn college degrees. I could not only read books but I could write them as well. Now I motivate and coach thousands of people worldwide on how to fill their lives with success and confidence.

It was easy to use my damaging past-life experiences as excuses to blame, shut down, and live in hopelessness rather than having the confidence to change and grow to create the fantastic life I desired.

I am now convinced, though, that the pains of the past have a purpose when we see them as teaching tools rather than excuses. As your confidence coach, I will guide you through an inner and outer revolution, and will show you how to use your disappointments and heartaches as *catalysts* to reinvent yourself, re-create your life, and become the person you have always wanted to be.

Regaining Our Confidence

When something predictable is removed or a sudden change happens in our personal lives or organizations, we tend to feel insecure and that produces stress. It is my opinion that almost 80 percent of the stress people feel in life is the result of two issues:

1. Confusion about decision making.
2. Lack of control in life due to unpredictable events.

With the wave of the Internet and smartphones, the world is now flat. What were once predictable business practices, predictable forms of communication, and predictable ways of working for predictable results have now become totally unpredictable.

CONFIDENCE COACHING SOLUTION
Confidence is a by-product of predictability.

The world is changing on many fronts at a rate faster than any generation has ever seen. Change is here to stay. Therefore, you have three choices:

1. Ignore it.
2. Work with it.
3. Make change happen and initiate progress.

Most people do the first, some do the second, but very few have the confidence to do the third. In order to stay up with technology and the new way of doing life and business, we must open our minds to learning new methods, embrace new ways of working, and be confident enough to engage a season of change in order to progress.

In a fast-changing, insecure, unpredictable world, your

confidence will not stay high automatically. If you are not careful, your confidence can change as quickly as your feelings change. You can feel like a champion one moment and then feel like a chump the next just by receiving a negative text message from a colleague or family member. Having a clear understanding of how to psychologically handle the changing events and circumstances in your life empowers you to maintain control in unpredictable times, reduce your stress, and produce the positive outcomes that you desire.

I first heard an initial insight on how events and reactions shape our outcomes at a Jack Canfield seminar. I adapted that insight into my own formula. Here is the formula I use with many of my coaching clients:

$$E + (C + R) = O$$

E is *Events*—You cannot control events. Throughout the day, you see, hear, and experience positive and negative events.

C is *Confidence Level*—Your confidence level determines whether you see the events in a positive or negative light. Is the challenge you face a problem or an opportunity?

R is *Reaction*—Your confidence level determines whether you react negatively (-) or positively (+) to the event you are facing.

O is *Outcome*—Your outcomes in life are going to be either positive or negative depending on your reaction to the events you see, hear, or experience throughout the day.

A client of mine, let's call him Dave, experienced an attack from one of his colleagues at work. This person vented her frustration and anger to my client's superiors about his inability to solve a problem. This work crisis had plunged him into depression and a serious lack of confidence.

After he shared with me the experience and his reaction, I shared this formula with him.

"Dave, where is your confidence (C) right now after this event (E)?"

"It's in the dirt, Keith."

I responded, "Your events (E) are beyond your control, but your confidence (C) and your reaction (R) to the events (E) are well within your control. If you lack confidence and react negatively, then the outcome (O) will be frustration, depression, and a growing lack of confidence."

"How can I change that?" Dave asked.

"Your confidence level can change if your perspective on the events changes. See the events as opportunities, not as problems. You have an opportunity to solve the problem and become a hero instead of a failure at work. Instead of defending yourself, attacking the colleague who attacked you, or making excuses, choose a confident, positive reaction," I said.

We then discussed the options and opportunities he had to solve the problem. His confidence and perception of his abilities began to strengthen as he talked. Seizing on the best solutions to his work crisis, he formulated a plan and presented it confidently (C) to his superiors, reacting (R) positively instead of becoming angry about the events (E) or defensive about his previous mistakes.

The outcome (O) equaled success. His superiors were impressed with his reaction and his solutions. They promoted him and demoted his attacker. This led to other promotions and success in his job and other opportunities beyond his work. Remember the formula. When events happen (E), you can add (+) to them your positive confidence and reaction (C+R) thus creating (=) an outcome (O) that brings success and increases your self-confidence. Again, here's the formula: E + (C+R) = O.

CONFIDENCE COACHING SOLUTION

*Confidence empowers you to take control
of your circumstances rather than allowing
the circumstances to control you.*

This current global economic crisis has affected many people. Some people, banks, car dealers, and businesses have greatly benefited from this crisis. The question is: *Are you falling into the trap of the negativity of the events that have happened, or are you staying confident and having the right response to this crisis so you can produce a great outcome?*

If you do not like the current outcomes that you are experiencing in your personal life or business, you have two decisions to make:

1. You can blame the negative events for the negative outcomes.

2. You can maintain your confidence and change your responses to the events until you get the outcomes you desire.

Six questions to ask yourself to achieve outrageously successful results in the midst of the most difficult times:

1. What current event do I need to acknowledge and define? You can never get the best out of an event by ignoring it or pretending that it is not there.

2. What are all of my response options? List all your possible response options, both positive and negative.

3. What is my *best* response option? Circle your best response option while you are in a confident state.

4. What *thoughts* are required for my best response actions? Control your thoughts by redefining the event for your own good.

5. What *words* are required for my best response actions? Words are the seedbed for your feelings, so make sure you are using confident talk.

6. What *actions* are required for my best response actions? Daily manage your best response with your best thoughts, words, and actions.

Since the negative news reports started rushing in at the end of 2007, my thoughts have been as follows: *This event is going to help me grow my business. People are going to need the message of confidence and success now more than ever.* I maintained my confidence, responded to this event in a positive way, and for the past two years I have had great years, and next year is promising to be even greater. Harvard Business School professor Rosabeth Moss Kanter comments on our times:

> *Sometimes it seems as if there are only two states of being: boom or bust. When things are up, it feels as if they will always be up. People come to believe they can succeed at anything they try; companies proffer grand visions of innovative futures; and investment is easy to attract. When things are down, it seems as if they will always be down. That's how depressed people feel; that's why recession-dominated economies find recovery elusive; that's why teams or businesses or schools can stay in decade-long slumps.*[1]

I live in the beautiful, sunny state of Florida, so I wear my sunglasses almost everywhere I go. Sometimes I forget to take off my sunglasses when I go into a restaurant or the mall. Occasionally, somebody will ask me "Why do you have your sunglasses on inside the building?"

I always respond by saying "It's because my future looks so bright I need sunglasses to block the glare."

1 Rosabeth Moss Kanter, *Confidence: How Winning Streaks & Losing Streaks Begin & End* (New York: Crown Business, 2006), p. 3.

The question you must ask yourself during times of economic challenges: *Am I focusing on Recession or Abundance?*

What do you see? *Recession or Abundance?*

What are you talking? *Recession or Abundance?*

How are you acting? *Recession or Abundance?*

What are you preparing for? *Recession or Abundance?*

Where your focus goes, your energy flows and your results show!

Confidence Is a By-Product of Predictability

I had a conversation with Bobb Biehl, one of my personal mentors, and insights emerged that he had written in his book:

When people first hear me say that "confidence is a by-product of predictability," I get many blank stares. You may have some questions too, so let me explain this principle with a "what if."[2]

I am a public speaker. A "what if" happened to me. I was diagnosed with a cyst in my jaw and had to have surgery. In the surgery, I had two molars and a wisdom tooth re-

2 Bobb Biehl, *Weathering the Midlife Storm: Map a Successful Course through Your Middle Years* (Wheaton, IL: Victor Books, 1996), p. 47.

moved, and part of my jawbone was replaced. Less than two weeks after the surgery, I stood up to speak and experienced unpredictability. Prior to the surgery, I had great confidence in my ability to speak. But after the surgery, I experienced feelings of uncertainty. Would I be able to talk for a full hour? Could I handle the pain that lingered from the surgery? Would I be able to talk distinctly? Would the stress of speaking increase the risk of infection? Everything was unpredictable as I stood up to speak. My confidence in speaking went from 90 percent certainty to 90 percent uncertainty. And this unpredictability caused my confidence to be challenged. Biehl reflects:

> As a result of the unpredictability, your confidence begins to wobble and droop, perhaps for the very first time in your adult life. The thing to remember is that this disillusionment is temporary. It feels at times as though it is permanent and will never again be remedied. But given a few months or years, you will find a new dream.[3]

What happened? My confidence was being challenged, but I chose to be confident in the face of unpredictability.

3 Ibid., p. 48.

Unpredictability creates "Loss of Control," producing the "Feeling of Stress." Predictability creates the feeling of "Being in Control," producing the "Feeling of Confidence."

You feel confident about yourself to the degree that you feel you are in control of your own life. The opposite is also true: You feel insecure about yourself to the degree that you feel you are not in control of your own life. To restore your confidence, you must jump-start. For me, I had to push myself to speak soon after my surgery and experience success—instead of stress—in order to restore the feeling of being in control. Are some things out of control in your life right now?

Do You Need a Jump Start?

I have noticed that every person, from CEOs to entry-level workers, has times when it seems like everything goes cold and their batteries go dead. The "Jump-Start Your Confidence Triangle" is your set of jumper cables during times when your confidence battery runs low and you need a quick boost to fire up your "outrageous success engine" again.

What was the first thing you did when your battery died? You asked somebody "Do you have jumper cables?" Asking the right question is the key to getting the solution you need for the immediate problems you are facing. It would be foolish for you to ask somebody to fill your car's gas tank if your battery was dead. The next triangle focuses on three important areas: questions, successes, and strengths.

1. ASK YOURSELF THE RIGHT QUESTIONS.

When we feel uncertain due to unpredictability in our lives, we may start asking ourselves the wrong questions, leading us down the slippery slope to losing our confidence. Confident people know the right questions to ask at the right times that will produce the solutions they need to reinvent themselves.

Profound questions produce profound answers. When feeling uncertain in the midst of unpredictable situations, ask yourself "What predictabilities have been removed from my life?" Then "What immediate action can I take to make my life more predictable?"

Confident people know how to simplify change and jump-start progress. They break up the steps to reinventing themselves into small, manageable steps.

A couple of my favorite questions that I ask myself during times of feeling insecure:

- What three things can I do in the next ninety days that will make a 50 percent difference in the remainder of this year?
- What one major problem do I need to solve that will make my life more predictable?

To jump-start your confidence, now is the time to start looking for solutions instead of focusing on problems. You must believe there is an answer to your current problems. If you confidently believe that there is an itinerary through the problems you are facing, your mind will find it. If you don't believe there is a solution, your mind will not create one.

When you start writing down some new ninety-day goals and action steps, you immediately become a different person. Your confidence toward yourself, your current challenges, and your future progresses in a very positive way. You start feeling more confident, optimistic, and more in control of your life.

2. LIST YOUR PRIOR AND PRESENT SUCCESSES.

One of the quickest ways to increase your confidence is to focus on the most positive and predictable areas of your life. When you focus on what is wrong with your life, you tend

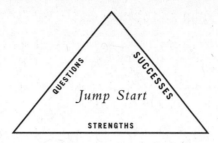

to feel discouraged. However, when you focus on what is right with your life, you start feeling encouraged.

Confident people exhibit a positive mental attitude. And confident leaders have reinvented themselves before—and they know they can do it again. You can too! You can increase your confidence by using your memory. Your mind is designed to recall past events. Great achievers learn to replay the memories of their past successes. You can actually use your past success to supercharge your confidence. Listing your former successes and accomplishments fuels your confidence to try again. Your list will empower you with the confidence to say, "I did this before; I can do it again."

By focusing on your successes, you start feeding the right emotion of confidence and you start starving the wrong emotions of fear, insecurity, and doubt.

Two natures beat within my breast,
The one is foul, the other is blessed.
The one I love, the other I hate,
The one I feed, will dominate.

—Unknown

3. FOCUS ON YOUR STRENGTHS.

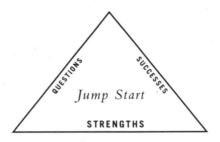

When the seasons of unpredictability enter our lives, we tend to forget about our strengths and are blinded to our own value, which is rooted in our strengths. When we focus on the problems, we overlook our possibilities. In unpredictable situations, one characteristic of a confident and successful leader is knowing how to deal with crisis, chaos, and change. Leaders have mastered the art of focusing on their strengths and what they do best.

So, when feeling uncertain, ask yourself *What are my greatest strengths?* You might not know right away, but simply ask yourself *What do I do that seems to be very easy for me, but is hard for others?* When you answer this question, you have discovered your single greatest strength. Design your life around your strengths and you will notice an instant confidence boost.

Confidence Transforms Crisis into Opportunity

What one person calls a crisis, another person calls an opportunity. No matter what challenges you face, remember that no one can stop you—but you. Confident people do not sit around waiting for someone or something to tell them what their future is going to look like—they create it. Leadership guru Peter Drucker said, "The best way to predict the future is to create it." Confident people are not fatalists. They take control of their situations instead of surrendering control to unpredictable circumstances, an unstable economy, or unreliable people. I suggest you do the same.

CONFIDENCE COACHING SOLUTION

The world will make a way for a person who
takes control and walks in confidence.

What is the difference between a singer who stands on stage and sings a song with a weak, trembling voice and one who sings the very same song with a strong, robust voice? One singer just sings and the other sings with confidence.

What is the difference between the number one salesperson and the mediocre salesperson? The mediocre salesperson just talks about the product; but the number one salesperson exudes confidence, expertise, and knowledge about the quality and benefits of buying the product.

Self-confidence is the first requisite to great undertakings.

—Samuel Johnson

What is the difference between the first-place Olympic athlete and the athlete who comes in tenth? The tenth-place Olympic athlete knows he or she is a good athlete; but the first-place athlete is confident that he or she is the "best" athlete.

Have you ever seen a person walking in supreme confidence? When such a person enters a room, the entire atmosphere changes. The person automatically lights up any gathering, attracting positive attention.

Watch the person as he or she deals with everyday problems. Listen to the way he or she talks on the telephone, stands, and sits, and notice how the person even leans forward slightly when listening to you. Confident people stand taller, sit straighter, and smile genuinely. Shake a confident person's hand and the grip will be firm, and he or she will look you directly in the eye.

Watch the movement of confident people's heads while they are speaking. They don't turn their heads from side to side as if saying no. When confident people talk, they move their heads up and down, confirming that "Yes, you can believe every word I am saying." When you shake your head from side to side while speaking, you are physically communicating that "No, I really don't mean what I am saying."

CONFIDENCE COACHING SOLUTION
*Champions are people in whom confidence
has become visible.*

Everything about a confident person creates an atmosphere that says "I am confident." It is important that everything you do or say projects an "I am confident, really confident" image.

Confidence is like a helpful virus spreading throughout your body. If you have it, it will infect everything you do in a positive way. If you don't, it will undermine everything you do.
—Dr. David Niven

Your personal aim and goal should be to deliberately and systematically create the circumstances that raise your confidence in everything you do. The most important question you can ask yourself is *How can I become more self-confident?*

CONFIDENCE COACHING SOLUTION
*Set as your personal goal: "I want
to increase my confidence!"*

It's time for you to move from where you are to increasing your personal confidence. You must come to a realization that you are the only one in this world who can do something about your own self-confidence. No one else can do it for you. Yes, someone else can coach you, but you must make the decision to start growing and changing. I can teach you how, but the work, sweat, and inner determination to create a habitual lifestyle of confidence is yours.

Build a Confidence Bridge

In addition to acting upon the confidence keys I have just given you, I want you to focus beyond where you are, where the economy is, or how other people regard you. When your focus is on "where you are," you've lost self-control and you're allowing negative outside events (E) or circumstances to undermine your confidence. What you need is a bridge from where you are to where you want to be.

CONFIDENCE COACHING SOLUTION

Confidence is the bridge between where
you are and where you want to be.

Where you are	Where you want to be
Who you are	Who you want to become
What you have	What you want
Whom you can help	Whom you want to help

It does not matter how successful you are at this moment, deep down inside you know there's a higher level of achievement for your personal and business life. When you stop reaching higher, you start sliding backward toward fear, uncertainty, and doubt (FUD).

Every new level is going to demand an increase of confidence in you and your team.

In my seminars I use this illustration:

Do you remember when you were an eighth grader? If so, do you remember how you felt as an eighth grader? You were on top.

However, when you graduated eighth grade and went to high school, although you went up another level, you were at the bottom of another level. You went from being the cool eighth grader to a peon freshman. Going to that new level tested all your confidence. You were thrust into a new environment. You went from a predictable schedule to an unpredictable schedule. Everything changed.

Gradually you climbed the ladder to become a senior. Do you remember how you felt as a senior? You were so confident you even had a Senior Skip Day when you and your classmates showed the peons and the teachers who was really in charge. But then you graduated from high school.

Some went to college; others went to work. You went up a level again, but you were at the bottom of it. You went from being a senior to being a freshman again, or perhaps you got a job, moved out of your parents' house, and experienced the pressure of paying your own bills.

The deception is that many times we think we are ready for the next level, but we really are not. The next level can destroy us if we do not have the confidence capacity to handle it.

Building our confidence before we leap to the next level is the key to not just obtaining what you want but also maintaining what you want.

It is one thing to obtain something; it requires confidence to maintain it.

To go to the next level, you must build your confidence to a higher level so you will have the capacity to handle the increased pressure of more responsibilities—the stress of making tougher decisions and the chaos that progress naturally produces. Confidence empowers you to endure the pain of rejection from those who want you to stay the same and from some who really want you to fail.

The gap between where you are and where you want to be will always demand a new level of confidence. If you are continually stretching yourself to maximize your full potential, you should never feel satisfied, content, or comfortable. Satisfaction and contentment with your current level of success kills your potential. When you get to the place where you are content with your latest accomplishments, you put yourself into a box of containment that keeps you from progressing to the next level.

As you move beyond the crisis of confidence into maximum self-confidence, I will walk you through some triangles of change that confront your present attitudes and challenge you to transform your thoughts, feelings, and behaviors with confidence. Change? Yes, I said *Change and initiate progress!* Let's move on and discover the number one enemy of confidence.

America's Confidence Coach Reminds You . . .

- Confidence empowers you to take control of your circumstances rather than allowing the circumstances to control you.
- Unpredictability creates "Loss of Control," producing the "Feeling of Stress." Predictability creates the feeling of "Being in Control," producing the "Feeling of Confidence."
- The world will make a way for a person who takes control and walks in confidence.
- Champions are people in whom confidence has become visible.
- Set your personal goal: I want to increase my confidence!
- Confidence is the bridge between where you are and where you want to be.

CONFIDENCE MAKEOVER STEPS NOW!

Answer the following questions:

1. What predictabilities have been removed from my life?
2. What immediate action can I take to make my life more predictable so I can reduce my stress?
3. What three things can I do in the next ninety days that will make a 50 percent difference in the rest of this year?
4. What one major problem do I need to solve that will make my life more predictable?
5. What are my five greatest achievements in the past?

   _____

   _____

   _____

   _____

   _____

6. Now that I have listed these successes, how am I feeling?
7. What is my greatest strength?
8. What do I do that seems to be very easy for me, but is hard for others?

Chapter 3

CONFRONTING YOUR FEAR, UNCERTAINTY, AND DOUBT!

Fear, uncertainty, and doubt are, and always have been, the greatest enemies of success and happiness.

—BRIAN TRACY,
America's leading business authority on success

WHEN I was a child, I remember playing a terrible trick on my younger brother. Before he went to bed one night, I quietly went into his room and hid in the closet. Later, after he was in bed, I started growling like a wolf, quietly at first and then I gradually increased my volume. He got really scared and yelled at the top of his voice for Mom. Our mother entered his room, opened the closet door, and found me. She said, "Look, it's only your brother Keith making that noise." My brother was very scared, but after receiving the revelation that it was just his big brother, he was instantly relieved.

The FUD wolf is making a lot of noise in the closets of most people today. He has been doing a lot of huffing and puffing, but he will never be able to blow your house down unless you let him. I want to open up the closet door and tell you "It's just the FUD wolf!"

There's an old German proverb that says something like "Fear makes the wolf bigger than he is."

Three questions every person and leaders of organizations and businesses should ask themselves:

- What stops people and organizations from moving forward, taking action, and creating the future they want and deserve?
- Why do people and organizations stay where they are?
- Why do human beings seem to resist change so much?

See if you can come up with your own conclusions after you hear a few of the conflicts some of my coaching clients have experienced over the years.

How FUD Stopped Success

- A very successful CEO . . . had a fear of implementing a proven sales process because he was afraid all his salespeople would quit the company.
- An abused woman . . . had a fear of leaving her husband because she was afraid she could not financially make it on her own.
- A doubting COO . . . worried about asking for a raise, even though he helped the company increase productivity and profits; he was afraid the boss would say no and fire him and get another COO.

- An overweight woman . . . who had been raped, had a fear of looking attractive, so she overate to keep men from looking at her.
- A stressed-out clergyman . . . would not fire a lazy and uncooperative associate pastor because he was afraid of the associate pastor's influence over the wealthy members of his church. He was afraid they would stop attending because they all liked the smooth-talking younger pastor.
- A professional athlete . . . doubted her ability to continue in the sport because of a few bad performances.
- An entrepreneur . . . would not put his house up for collateral because he was uncertain about the success of his company.
- A network-marketing businesswoman . . . was afraid to talk to others about her business opportunity because she was afraid people would label her as a weird person who is into one of those "get-rich-quick pyramid schemes."
- A single man . . . would not ask a woman whom he had dearly loved for ten years out on a date because he was afraid of rejection.
- A struggling salesperson . . . closed a meager 15 percent of his sales while other salespeople in the company were closing 35 to 50 percent. His number one problem was closing a deal. When it was time to ask the client to make the order, he was afraid to ask for their business and lost most of his sales.

❀ A professional speaker . . . was afraid to fly. Why? Because he had a dream he died in an airplane crash.

After reading these stories, what would you say is stopping people and organizations from progress and reinvention? FEAR! UNCERTAINTY! DOUBT! Fear is the mother who keeps birthing children of uncertainty and doubt. Again, fear breeds uncertainty and doubt—the FUD disease.

Airplane crashes do happen. However, the chances are higher that a person will die in a car crash than in an airplane crash. Because of the professional speaker's personal fears, he traveled all across the United States in a motor home. Can you believe that? That is almost like traveling in a horse and buggy in the twenty-first century. When international invitations to speak came into his office, he had to decline very influential and prosperous opportunities.

CONFIDENCE COACHING SOLUTION
❀ ━━━━━━━━━━━━━━━━━━━━━━━━━━━━━ ❀
*Fear intimidates its victim by painting a
negative picture of future outcomes.*

Fear of flying, or whatever fear you may have, immobilizes your potential because it severely limits you from going to the next level. More important, fear severely slows down your speed of achievement. In the twenty-first century, you cannot afford to be traveling at the speed of horse and buggy when you are competing with people who are traveling by jumbo jet.

The opposite of fear is CONFIDENCE.

CONFIDENCE COACHING SOLUTION

Confidence is the power to achieve extraordinary results.

Let's look at the three forces that are working together to erode your confidence levels and stop you from taking massive action so you can achieve the results you want and deserve out of life.

The Force of Fear

Fear roars like a lion behind the closed door of the room where all your dreams reside. If you have the confidence to open the door, you will suddenly discover it was not a lion, just a whimpering pussycat with a big microphone. The roar of fear tries to intimidate you, belittle you, and deceive you. Fear presents itself as a larger-than-life giant who is standing in your way, trying to make you feel as helpless as a little grasshopper who must gracefully bow and back away or be trampled by the giant's foot. Fear is the bully who's still chasing you around on the playground of life.

Fear's seduction is powerful, always trying to lure you away from your date with confidence that will lead you to the life of your dreams. Fear romances your insecurities and your self-doubts, trying to get you to jump into bed with it. The more familiar you become with its kiss, the easier it is to condition you to stay in its bed and never leave. Fear serves cookies of comfort, security, and safety. Don't be deceived; each cookie is laced with a venomous poison that will gradually eat away your confidence and destroy your dreams.

The Force of Uncertainty

I have insecurities. But whatever I'm insecure about, I don't dissect it, but I'll go after it and say, "What am I afraid of?" I bet the average successful person can tell you they've failed so much more than they've had success. I've had far more failures than I've had successes. With every commercial I've gotten, there were two hundred I didn't get. You have to go after what you're afraid of.

—Kevin Sorbo, actor

Life is full of uncertainties. Our culture is constantly changing, which causes uncertainty. I experience uncertainty every week as I travel on airlines throughout the world. Will this plane take off on time? Will it arrive on time? Will the next plane take off on time? Will that plane land on time? What was that weird noise? Is this plane safe for travel?

One day the stock market can be up, the next day it can be down. One year the area you live in can have a mild winter, the next year your area sets records for snow accumulation. One year while I was living in Florida, we had no hurricanes, the next year we experienced three hurricanes. You don't know if the sun will shine today, or if it will be cloudy and rainy. You can never be certain how people will treat you. Your spouse can be your greatest supporter one day and want to divorce you the next day.

There are uncertainties in the marketplace. Toys that are in demand during Christmastime one year can be obsolete the next year. Technology changes quickly. Personal communication devices and electronic toys seem to be updated monthly. Fashion changes like the wind. What was in style one season can be totally out of style the next season. Whenever a culture is experiencing progress and change, you will have to deal with the forces of uncertainty.

Your outer world will always be filled with uncertainty, which can produce stress. However, you do not have to allow your inner world to be full of uncertainty. You can live in a state of supreme confidence in uncertain times.

Uncertainty is rooted in a number of factors. You may be uncertain of yourself—your knowledge, skills, or abilities. Or you may be uncertain of those around you—their abilities, commitment, or support of you. You may also be uncertain of the outcomes of your future. Fearing failure, success, or the unknown often prompts uncertainty. Yet the only way to fail for sure is to quit.

ARE YOU STOPPED BY YOUR START?

Life is filled with starts and stops. What stops people? What keeps people from achieving their goals, obtaining success, and living the life of their dreams? I am convinced that most people are stopped by the start. The first step to changing your life or business always creates a high level of uncertainty. The first step is always the hardest and that's why so few people take the step. Uncertainty says, "It is easier to step back from a challenge. Just wait until the conditions are better." Uncertainty tries to seduce you with procrastination by painting a picture of a negative outcome if you take the first step.

Brian Tracy makes this powerful statement:

How many times do you think that people try to achieve their new goals before they give up? The average is less than one time. Most people give up before they even make the first try. And the reason they give up is because of all the obstacles, difficulties, problems, and roadblocks that immediately appear as soon as they decide to do something that they have never done before. The fact is that successful people fail far more often than unsuccessful people. Successful people try more things, fall down, pick themselves up, and try again—over and over again—before they finally win. Unsuccessful people try a few things, if they try at all, and very soon quit and go back to what they were doing before.[1]

1 Brian Tracy, *Goals! How to Get Everything You Want—Faster Than You Ever Thought Possible* (San Francisco: Berrett-Koehler Publishers, 2003), p. 107.

Often counselors use a tool called "the worst-case scenario." This tool is used to get you to face your fears and uncertainties. What if the worst-case scenario happens? If you can imagine it, you can also plan and prepare to minimize its possibility. Don't let uncertainty paralyze you; let it motivate you to plan a strategy to eliminate or minimize all the undesirable outcomes so that the odds for your success far outweigh any possibilities of failure.

YOUR UNCERTAINTIES ARE ROOTED IN YOUR INSECURITIES

Uncertainty is not an indication of poor leadership . . . the temptation is to think, "If I were a good leader, I would know exactly what to do." Increased responsibility means dealing with more and more intangibles and, therefore, more complex uncertainty. Leaders can afford to be uncertain, but we cannot afford to be unclear. People will not follow fuzzy leadership.

—Andy Stanley, megachurch pastor

We are uncertain because we are insecure. We doubt ourselves. Right now there may be something you are not seeing that is keeping you from getting to where you want to go. Sometimes just a small adjustment can bring about great changes in your future.

One of the greatest challenges you will ever face in your personal life is identifying insecurities in yourself that can be keeping you from achieving the things you really want in life.

If my guess is right, it is easy for you to identify insecurities, fears, poor self-image, low self-esteem, and lack of confidence in those who are close to you. Have you ever made one of these statements about someone: "Can't they see how they are sabotaging their own success? Can't they see what dumb mistakes they keep making over and over again?" I guess this is why the old proverb is so true: "There is a way that seems right to a man, But its end is the way of death."[2] Your own personal blind spots, wrong self-perceptions, prejudices, or assumptions may be your greatest obstacles.

We all have what I call "blind spots." These blind spots are issues within ourselves that we can't see, but they are keeping us from the success we really want and deserve in our lives. Other people in your life are well aware of these blind spots. However, we don't see them ourselves. Sadly, most people surround themselves with people who will just accept them for who they are and never challenge them to change for the better. Unfortunately, many times people who are at a higher level than we are end up leaving our circle of friends and colleagues; we end up surrounded by people who are at the same level—who accept one another the way they are.

I don't want a bunch of people around me who will not tell me my underarms stink! Do you? I want to be confident enough to allow my real friends to bring out the best in me

2 Proverbs 16:25 (NKJV).

without my getting offended. Do you? Ken Blanchard taught me that "feedback is the breakfast of champions."

The Force of Doubt

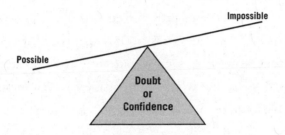

Do you remember playing on a teeter-totter when you were a kid? I remember the first time I played on one at school with one of my friends at recess. We went back and forth . . . up and down. We did this so many times I started to get dizzy and then I got sick and lost my lunch in the toilet.

Doubt is like a teeter-totter; it bounces back and forth so much that your mind gets fuzzy, dizzy, and confused. Do you keep asking yourself, "Am I making the right decision?" This reveals that doubt has entered your decision-making process. I have found that when I gather all the facts and they are clear, the decision-making process becomes easier and doubt loses its grip.

CONFIDENCE COACHING SOLUTION

*Doubt says, "What if I fail?" Confidence
says, "What if I succeed?"*

The force and power of doubt lies in its ability to interrogate you. Doubt is the prosecuting attorney who takes your confidence to court and tries to convince you that your outcomes will be negative. Doubt constantly asks: What if it will happen . . . what if it won't? Is it possible . . . is it impossible? Am I able to do this . . . will I fail? What if my plan does not work out . . . what if it does? What if the client does not like my product . . . what if they love my product? Should I ask her for a date . . . should I not ask her for a date? Will he say yes . . . or will he say no? Vacillating questions infuse doubt and never reveal answers.

Whatever side gets the most focus or weight in your mind determines if you are in confidence or doubt. If your mind stays focused on the possibilities, you will win the teeter-totter match. If you allow your mind to be weighed down

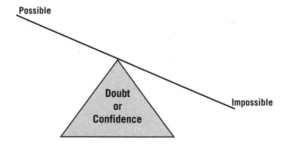

with why things cannot happen, with all the impossibilities, you lose the teeter-totter match and will live in doubt and do without. Doubt stops you from unleashing your possibilities and living your life to the fullest.

How do you get a confident person to doubt? You simply ask them a question. In my seminars, I use this example all the time. I pull a person out of the crowd and start asking that person some questions.

For example, if the person has black hair, I ask, "Do you have black hair?" The person will immediately answer "Yes." Then I ask, "Are you one hundred percent sure you have black hair?" Then the person hesitates and begins to think about the question. At that moment, I have introduced the power of doubt into the thinking process.

Next, I show the group how the person responded with confidence the first time. However, when I probed deeper using another question and doubt as my tool, the person hesitated and did not respond with confidence.

Doubt does this; it keeps asking you the nagging negative questions and tries to move you from a confident state to a doubting state. Staying in this negative state causes you to go back and forth like an emotional roller coaster and produces more stress, anxiety, and confusion, which increase your fears, uncertainties, and doubts (FUD).

Use doubt as a tool to your advantage by asking this question: "Am I certain my doubts are legitimate?" Use doubt to doubt your doubts. A wise axiom teaches "Starve your doubts, feed your faith, and see positive results."

The force of doubt is here to stay. The "what ifs" and the "maybe, maybe nots" will always try to turn your confidence into Silly Putty.

How to Overcome FUD

How do you move from fear, uncertainty, and doubt into supreme confidence?

You can learn to live in a state of supreme confidence. When you are in a confident state, you become FUD-less. After years of coaching peak performers, I have no doubt in my mind that fear is the greatest enemy to success. Why? Because fear is a powerful force at work within you that blinds you to your strengths, skills, and abilities. Fear undermines positive attitudes and accomplishments within you. It replaces confidence with a variety of fears that paralyze and cripple positive thinking and successful actions.

The first step in overcoming anything is to identify the enemy you are fighting against. How can you win the fight if you do not know who your enemy is?

Fight or Flight

When human beings and animals are faced with challenges, attacks, threats, or something that is trying to destroy them, they have one of two responses. They either fight or they take flight. Sadly, most people cower away from obstacles and challenges and choose the option of flight. Most people are conditioned by our culture to be nice rather than fight. It is sad; many men have been tamed to the point where they don't even act like strong, protective men anymore. When a challenge comes, they act like pussycats instead of lions, in my opinion.

We are conditioned to try to lead like lambs instead of lions. I have seen far too many people walk away from what rightfully belonged to them and miss out on success. I have seen too many people stop fighting for what they really want just before they achieve it. You must see obstacles, challenges, and attacks as a fight to be fought so you can claim victory over your enemy.

Confidence is what empowers a person to keep fighting when the going gets tough. Wealth and success favor the confident. Success rarely rewards the timid! Don't confuse humility with timidity.

An enemy gives you a reason to fight. Engaging in warfare challenges your level of confidence, competence, and character. It forces you to get out of your comfort zone and exercise your untapped potential, talents, and abilities. Without a fight, you can become fat, lazy, and complacent. In this state, you can easily lose your dreams, purpose, passion, and inner fire.

Want to really get fired up? Find an enemy and pick a fight.

Here is an example. I am working hard to empower leaders with more confidence so they can experience outrageous success in life and business. I want to help people restore their confidence, self-image, self-esteem, self-worth, and self-respect so they can live meaningful and happy lives.

What is my enemy?

* Fear
* Uncertainty
* Doubt

Want to ignite your own motivation? Find an enemy and pick a fight. A great place to start is with the FUD in your life and organization. Let me help you out. What do you hate? I mean, really hate? What makes you mad? What makes you want to punch something? Be like Rocky when he put a picture of Apollo on his training-room mirror, find your enemy, and let that image stir your blood—dig a little deeper, go a little longer, and fight harder.

Don't pray, wish, or try to ignore your enemy away. Conquer it! The enemy you conquer is the one who will make you famous. Remember, Goliath made David famous. Like my mentor John Kelly says, "Achievement always demands warfare!"

What's Stopping You?

What stops you from moving forward . . . taking action . . . becoming your best? The answer is *fear*. Fear can destroy your psychology and immobilize you. To change your life, you *must* learn to face your fears.

The top seven confidence-destroying poisons that you will face on the road to success:

1. Fear that I'm not good enough
2. Fear that I won't be loved
3. Fear of success
4. Fear of failure
5. Fear of rejection
6. Fear of taking a risk
7. Fear of the unknown

Let's dissect each confidence poison separately.

CONFIDENCE ENEMY #1: FEAR THAT I'M NOT GOOD ENOUGH

This enemy tries to tempt you into believing the lie that you are not good enough. You don't have enough skill, good looks, intelligence, talent, time, strength, money, or creativity to accomplish your dream or vision. If you wait until you think you are good enough, you will never take the next step. If you do not take the first step, you will live your life in regret, wondering if you could have achieved more in life.

CONFIDENCE ENEMY #2: FEAR THAT I WON'T BE LOVED

Fear of not being loved tries to convince you that people will not love you and accept you and will instead reject you, make fun of you, mock and ridicule you, and this keeps you from making the changes you need to achieve outrageous success. So then what? Why allow others to keep you from moving forward? You will never be able to please everyone in your life. But pleasing yourself by becoming successful will influence others in a good way so you can help them build their dream. But first you have to take charge of and fulfill your dream, your desire, your vision, your life, and your next step. Do it because it's right; it's your purpose and destiny. Step out and you will be surprised how many people will want to follow.

CONFIDENCE ENEMY #3: FEAR OF SUCCESS

Yes, many people are actually afraid of becoming successful. I thought that everybody wanted to be a success, but then I learned that many people actually sabotage their own success just to stay at a comfortable, mediocre level. People who fear success can sometimes appear to be very humble or modest and may even show disgust with others who are highly confident.

They feel unworthy and undeserving of higher levels of success and achievement. One of the most frequent messages created by the fear of success is "I do not deserve to earn more money," or "What will people think of me if I become really successful?" Not using their talents and skills to the fullest robs society—and their families—of the additional resources that could be shared for the betterment of others.

CONFIDENCE ENEMY #4: FEAR OF FAILURE

The fear of failure keeps you from attempting to do the things that you have always longed to do. Fear of failure keeps you stuck at a job that you hate or at a dead-end job that is leading you nowhere. The fear of failure stops you from making forward progress in your life or business. The fear of failure keeps businesses from launching out into new markets. What have you always wanted to do but have been too afraid to attempt?

Did you know that entrepreneurs almost never get their first business off the ground? Or their second? Or their third? According to some researchers, the average is 3.8 failures before entrepreneurs finally make it in business.

They are not deterred by problems, mistakes, or errors. Why? Because they don't see setbacks as failures. They recognize that three steps forward and two steps back still equals one step forward. As a result, they overcome the average and become achievers. You can too!

CONFIDENCE ENEMY #5: FEAR OF REJECTION

Who is the most powerful person in the world? Some would say the president of the United States. And I would have to agree. However, although Barack Obama received more votes than his opponent, almost sixty million people rejected him by not voting for him.[3] Everyone you meet is afraid of both failure and rejection to some degree. Fear of rejection is one of the most common fears shared by all human beings. Nobody wants to be turned down, put down, left out, kicked out, disliked, or unwanted. Everybody wants to be loved, accepted, respected, cared for, and valued.

CONFIDENCE ENEMY #6: FEAR OF TAKING A RISK

Confident people are risk takers. They boldly step out of their boring comfort zones and decide to live life in the excitement of the adventure zone. The greatest defeat in life is to never risk a thing.

People who are afraid of taking a risk attempt nothing, have nothing, and can only be nothing. They avoid risky situations, pressures, criticism, and suffering, and although they may escape the feelings of disappointment, they will never really live, learn, grow, or change. They become caged prisoners in their own comfort zones, held captive by their own inner doubts and fears.

CONFIDENCE ENEMY #7: FEAR OF THE UNKNOWN

People who are afraid of the unknown are always unsure of themselves and face a lack of confidence when they are dealing

3 "United States Presidential Election, 2008," Wikipedia, http://en.wikipedia.org/wiki/United_States_presidential_election,_2008#General_election_campaign.

with the unknown. Watch a mechanic try to repair the engine of a strange automobile that he does not understand. He hesitates. His every movement shows lack of confidence.

Then watch a master mechanic who understands the engine he is repairing. His every movement exudes confidence. It is the same for anything we are facing. The more we know about it, the more confidence we will have in dealing with it.

From Ordinary to Extraordinary

The history of the human race is filled with stories about ordinary people who have overcome their fears and accomplished extraordinary things. You must realize that fear is hardwired into every human being—nothing you do in your lifetime will take fear away. The secret is learning how to use fear instead of letting fear use you.

A popular acronym is F.E.A.R.

F = Fantasized
E = Experiences
A = Appearing
R = Real

Here is an exercise I walk my clients through:

I want to _____, but I am afraid _____ will happen if I do.

The second blank is the fantasized (F) experience (E). This is the negative outcome that you have imagined in your own mind that stops you from taking action so you can be, do, and have what you really want in life.

Let me give you an example. When my speaking business was starting to really grow and we began selling a few of my books and tapes after presentations, a few people would come to the table and ask if they could purchase our material by credit card. During those days, we did not have the ability to accept credit cards. The requests over the next year increased so I called the credit card company to find out how we could start accepting credit card payments for our products. I found out that it would cost $19.95 per month for a service charge.

So here is how I would fill in the blanks: I want to <u>start accepting credit cards</u>, but I am afraid <u>I will lose money</u> every month if I do.

What was my desire? I wanted to start accepting credit cards.

What was my fantasized experience? I would lose money every month.

Where was my focus? I was more focused on what I would lose versus what I would gain. Fear of loss started controlling my mind instead of focusing my thoughts on the opportunity for outrageous success.

What happened after I made the decision to accept credit

card payments? Our product sales quadrupled. We sold more products after one keynote message than I did in an entire month before I accepted credit cards.

Yet I remember agonizing back and forth for months about this no-brainer decision. I look back now and laugh at myself. *What in the world was I thinking?* Well, I wasn't thinking, I was *fantasizing* the negative instead of *visualizing* the positive.

Ask yourself *What is the fantasized experience I am imagining in my mind, and how can I replace the picture of failure with a new picture of outrageous success?*

New Focus: I want to start accepting credit cards because I will quadruple my product sales.

What's your New Focus?

Negative Thinking Patterns

We are the by-products of our own thoughts. What we think about most expands. If our thoughts are focused on a negative outcome, they will expand and become a living reality. Fear is all about dwelling on what could go *wrong* instead of what can go *right*.

Fear keeps you from going to where you want to go. Confident people refuse to allow their minds to play negative movies of a future that they do not want. In order to maximize your life, you must neutralize fear with CONFIDENCE.

The person who fears to act will never know what he or

she could have done. Outrageously successful entrepreneur Donald Trump remarked:

> *Recently, an interviewer asked me what my greatest fears were. I said I didn't have any. He seemed surprised, but this is how I see it: If you label something as a fear, then it creates fear when sometimes it's not a fear, but a concern. For example, I know just as well as everyone else that New York City experienced a major terrorist attack, and the thought of that is a concern for all of us because it affects all of us. It's happened in many places, so it's a worldwide concern. But if we let it become a firmly rooted fear, then terrorists will have won.*[4]

Confront Your FUD!

I have mentioned a few fear poisons that kill confidence. Now I want to invite you to complete a self-test. By each of the poisons listed, write a 0 (feel this least) to a 10 (for most strongly felt).

___Fear of failure

___Fear of rejection

___Fear of success

___Fear of embarrassment

4 Donald J. Trump, *Think Like a Champion: An Informal Education in Business and Life* (New York: Vanguard Press, 2009), p. 51.

___Fear of being wrong

___Fear of taking a risk

___Fear of not being loved

___Fear of not being good enough

___Fear of exposure

___Fear of not knowing

___Fear of being unprepared

___Fear of others

___Fear of consequences

___Fear of not looking right

___Fear of saying the wrong thing

___Fear of criticism

___Fear of being alone

_____ Total

Total your score. The lower your total score, the lower your FUD. If you scored over thirty, you are in the Confidence Emergency Room!

Now circle the three fears that paralyze you the most. Are you willing to transform these into simple concerns and move forward? Fear paralyzes; concern admits the possibility but moves forward in an informed, reasonable way.

Now that you have started to confront the FUD in your life, it's time to take the necessary steps in overcoming it. We'll now turn to practical and effective ways to defeat the fear, uncertainty, and doubt that can attack you any day and in various, devious ways.

America's Confidence Coach Reminds You . . .

- Confidence is the power to achieve extraordinary results.
- Fear intimidates its victim by painting a negative picture of future outcomes.
- Doubt says, "What if I fail?" Confidence says, "What if I succeed?"
- The voices of fear, uncertainty, and doubt will always try to scream louder than the quiet voice of confidence.
- Identify your enemy.

Confidence Enemy #1: Fear that I'm Not Good Enough

Confidence Enemy #2: Fear that I Won't Be Loved

Confidence Enemy #3: Fear of Success

Confidence Enemy #4: Fear of Failure

Confidence Enemy #5: Fear of Rejection

Confidence Enemy #6: Fear of Taking a Risk

Confidence Enemy #7: Fear of the Unknown

CONFIDENCE MAKEOVER STEPS NOW!

1. Which confidence key do you need to apply in your life right now, and how will you practice it?

2. Which poison affects you most now, and what will you do about it? When will you take action?

3. When fear attacks, list the first three thoughts you will embrace to counteract its poison:

_____

_____

_____

Chapter 4

OVERCOMING FUD WITH CONFIDENCE

Every moment of your life you are
making three decisions:
1. What are you going to focus on?
2. What does that mean to you?
3. What are you going to do about it?

—ANTHONY ROBBINS,
speaking at a conference

THESE days I speak to crowds of thousands about leadership and confidence with very little fear, uncertainty, and doubt (FUD). But on June 14, 1990, I gave my very first speech in front of a huge crowd of seven people on a Wednesday night at a small country church in Tarpon Springs, Florida. The week prior to my speech was one of the most miserable weeks of my life. Why? Because I was focusing on the negative outcome of how terrible that speech would be. I could not eat. I was up-tight. Negative thoughts controlled my mind as I continually rehearsed these questions: *What if I fail? What if I say the wrong words? What if I forget what I want to say? What if people do not like what I have to say? I don't know anything about the Bible. What can a twenty-three-year-old tell a bunch of life-seasoned people about God?*

The day I was to speak, I was a basket case. My palms were sweaty all day and my stomach felt like it was doing somersaults, which caused diarrhea. I was petrified. My mind was focused on the speaking engagement being a total flop. A few minutes before I was supposed to speak, I had to rush to the bathroom again. While I was sitting on the toilet, the forces of FUD gripped my mind. For a moment, I wanted to run to my car and go home.

I suddenly realized at that moment that I had spent the entire week focusing on this event in a negative way. In that moment, the battle for my future as a professional speaker was on. Who was going to win the fight—Mr. Confidence or Mr. FUD? I made my first decision to change my focus to a positive outcome. What if my message turned out great? What if somebody's life was changed by what I communicated? What if I actually communicated my message in a powerful way? After all, I had been preparing my first speech for more than three months.

It was time to get off the toilet!

I made my second decision and changed my thinking about what this opportunity meant to me. *This is my opportunity to start building my motivational skills as a speaker. I have an opportunity to share how I was able to change my life! I have been allowing fear, uncertainty, and doubt to rob me of my confidence.* Then I made my third decision based on what Anthony Robbins said. I asked myself *What am I going to do about it?* I decided to step into fear, march into the room of seven people, and deliver my speech with great passion and confidence.

The result was incredible! Everybody loved the message. I was then asked by the pastor to give a speech every Wednesday night and the crowd grew as people from the community came to hear what I had to say.

I am motivated by fear. I hate being scared to do something. What developed in my early days was the attitude that I started attacking things I was scared of.[1]

—Will Smith

Confronting and attacking your fears, uncertainties, and doubts (FUD) is the cost of going to the next level. Overcoming FUD must become a priority in your life. My responsibility as your coach is to help you face your FUD and overcome them. How do professional people such as police officers and firefighters, who face danger every day, do it?

Police officers and firefighters deal with fear on a daily basis. The fear of death hits them every time they prepare to arrest a drug dealer or enter a burning building. Just before they go into action, they experience the feelings of fear and uncertainty—not knowing whether they will survive or not.

However, the force of fear is destroyed when that police officer takes the first action step to knock down the door of a drug dealer's house or the firefighter takes that first step into

1 "Will's Wisdom," YouTube, http://www.youtube.com/watch?v=OLN2k0b3g70.

the burning building to save a child. They literally step into fear with confidence, and because they do, the fear disappears. They are totally focused on the reward of capturing the crooks or saving a person's life. *By confronting their fears, they can focus on the immediate situation and get the job done.*

Confrontation breeds discomfort and this is the reason why most people ignore it. However, discomfort is the cost of going to the next level. What you tolerate or are comfortable with, you cannot change. Whatever you don't confront, you are willing to tolerate. You can only change when you hate the present FUD. You must hate the present FUD and make changes today to qualify for a greater future.

Take the Next Step and Overcome FUD

FUD create a mental block that will stop you from moving forward. FUD are a paralysis that stops you from creating a solution to your problems. They stop creative thinking. An antidote to FUD is as simple as confidently taking the next step—taking action, doing something positive, creative, innovative, and assertive.

Overcoming FUD is a decision to claim destiny over past experiences, small steps forward instead of passive steps backward—moving up instead of sitting down.

Ready to overcome your FUD? Here's the Achiever's Triangle to help you find your traction so you can take massive action.

Point 1: Outrageous Confidence

Let me illustrate how this Achiever's Triangle works to overcome your FUD with a story from my childhood.

My grandfather had an effective way of dealing with any fears, uncertainties, and doubts that I had as a kid. For instance, I was very afraid of my grandparent, horse when I was a young boy. But one day my grandfather, exuding confidence, finally convinced me to at least get up on the horse and feel what it was like to "sit on the horse." As soon as I got on the horse, my grandfather slapped the horse hard on its rear end. That horse took off running as fast as it could across a ten-acre Indiana cornfield. I was able to hang on for the first four hundred yards and then down to the ground I went. I picked myself up off the ground and was ready to go on another exciting ride. All my FUD about riding that horse suddenly vanished that day when my grandfather forced me to face my FUD with action.

Another day I was at my grandparents' lake cottage. I was afraid of the water, so I would not go swimming with the other kids. Once again, Grandpa had a way of curing my FUD. He gathered us together to go for a ride around the lake in a pontoon boat. As soon as we got close to the beach on the lakeshore, he threw me into the water and off he went across the lake in the boat. I thought I was going to drown that day. However, I made it to the shore and from that day on I was not afraid of the water. Once again, when I was forced to confront my FUD with corresponding action, my FUD were released!

Point 2: Outrageous Actions

The two greatest fear busters are knowledge and action.
—Denis Waitley, best-selling author, speaker,
and high-performance consultant

One of the fastest growing religions of our century is Christianity. Whether you believe in Jesus Christ or not, one thing you cannot deny is the success of this movement that has produced the largest religion in the world. Most religions are based on the philosophies of their leaders. The early success of Christianity is revealed in one of the most powerful books in the Bible—the Book of Acts! This book historically heralds the outrageous success of the first disciples of Christ. When you read this book, you become amazed at how the first-century leaders risked their lives, worked really hard, and took massive action to spread worldwide their philosophy about Jesus being the Son of God.

They did not just write a theology, talk about what was going to happen, make false promises, or theorize on how to turn the world upside down. They took outrageous actions that resulted in their dying violently in coliseums, being torn apart by wild animals, being beaten and crucified, and being literally torched with fire. They went out and demonstrated their faith by their actions. It is amazing how fast this small group of people spread their message around the world without the use of television, telephones, the Internet, e-mails, Twitter, Facebook, or radios. The Book of Acts models what we need to do—*act outrageously!*

Point 3: Outrageous Rewards

Do you sometimes feel as if nobody is in your corner cheering you on as you fight through life to achieve your dreams? If so, you are not alone. Self-mastery requires the skill of having the ability to keep yourself motivated. There are times in life when nobody is going to be in your ring cheering you on to victory. You cannot depend on the government, your spouse, your family, your friends, or your boss to motivate you.

Who is the world's greatest motivator? Just look into the mirror. Yes! The greatest motivator in the world is *you*! Nobody, and I mean *nobody*, can motivate you like you can.

Motivation is the psychological feature that arouses an organism to action toward a desired goal. The root word of motivation is motive, which simply means a reason for doing something.

How can you motivate yourself enough to take action? Realize your rewards.

REWARDS—THE FORCE OF MOTIVATION

Focusing on the rewards you will attain if you face your FUD and take action is the key to self-motivation. Rewards do not just go to everybody. Rewards are passed out to those who achieve extraordinary results. They go to those whose performance and results are better than everybody else's. At the Olympics, only the top three finishers get to stand on the platform and be honored to receive the gold, silver, and bronze medals. Champions in athletics, business, and life do the disciplines necessary to achieve these extraordinary results. Rewards are reserved for those who are willing to do what the majority of the world is unwilling to do.

Affirmation without discipline is delusion.[2]

—Jim Rohn

Outrageous rewards are more than just "needs." Rewards are the things you really "want" out of life. Mere needs do not motivate you.

Here's an example. My wife went to Wal-Mart the other day and she came back with several bags of groceries. When she walked into the house, she said, "I got you a surprise." I don't know about you, but I love surprises! My energy levels almost instantly increased. As I waited with great anticipation, she reached in the bag and pulled out a box of toothpaste. Needless to say, my excitement levels dropped instantly. Then she said, "I got something else for you." I knew it had to be better than toothpaste. She then reached in the bag and pulled out deodorant. Again my heart and energy levels sank. Then she said, "I have something else for you." My thought was that the next thing had to be better than toothpaste and deodorant. She reached in the bag and pulled out a package of toilet paper. I sincerely thanked her for getting my toiletries—things I "need."

Question. Did getting my needs met motivate me, energize me, fire me up to go change the world? NO!

2 "Beginning Quotes," Brainy Quote, http://www.brainyquote.com/quotes/keywords/beginning_2.html.

Rewards are not needs, they are wants. Your wants or personal heart's desires are what really supercharge you to break through the walls of fear so you can obtain the things you really want for your life and business.

For example, I always "wanted" a canary yellow Corvette convertible. I didn't necessarily "need" one; any car could have taken me from point A to point B. However, because I wanted one, I would frequently drive by the Chevrolet dealer very slowly so I could see all the Corvettes for sale. I kept my eyes on my desired outcome. I would say to myself, *One of these days I'm going to buy a yellow Corvette. I'm going to keep taking action until I can get the reward.* This motivated me to work hard to build my speaking and coaching business. I will never forget the day I drove past the dealership and right out front was my yellow Corvette convertible sparkling in the Florida sun. I went home and told my wife about the car. She was excited and said, "Why don't you go buy it? We have the money for it."

When I drove the car off the lot, I felt like I was in heaven. I was so energized to break through some more walls and achieve even greater things in my life and business.

KEEP YOUR EYES ON THE PRIZE

I am not a television watcher. However, my favorite television show is *Fear Factor*. I love this show because most of the contestants model the force of confidence. This show teaches us the powerful principle of focus. What would cause a person to eat cow eyes, African cave spiders, and eggs with baby chickens inside? What would cause a person to jump off the top of one speeding semitrailer onto another, reach his or her hand into a fish tank with electric eels, or get into a box the size of a coffin and have snakes, scorpions, and roaches poured on them?

First, it is the reward of winning. Second, it is the reward of $50,000 if they win. These people have learned the art of confronting their greatest fears with action by keeping their focus on the future rewards that overcoming their fears will produce. I have found that people are motivated to action in three basic ways:

Motivator 1. *Incentive* based on rewards. Your boss says, "Whoever sells the most products today will receive a $1,000 bonus."

Motivator 2. *Fear* based on punishment. Your boss says, "If you do not sell your quota today, you are fired."

Motivator 3. *Greatness* based on the possibility of who you can become—a champion! Your boss says, "You have the ability to be the number one salesperson this month."

When I first started working as a professional speaker, I thought I could just send out marketing material and people would start calling me out of the blue to have me speak at their business or organization.

I sat by my phone . . . and I sat by my phone . . . and nobody, and I mean nobody, called me. Thankfully a friend of mine, who is also in the speaking business, told me clients will rarely, if ever, call you. He also taught me that the main thing a new speaker had to do was make phone calls to potential clients and "sell himself." I instantly thought, *I hate cold calling. I hate being rejected. I can't do it.* However, my next thought was *If I don't get some speaking engagements really fast, I am not going to be able to put food on the table.*

The reward of food being on the table and my bills being paid moved me to overcome my fear of rejection. So I picked up the telephone and started calling potential clients. My friend told me that I would need to make about twenty calls in order to book one client. I decided that I was not going to focus on the rejections that I was going to receive.

Instead, I chose to focus on the reward of landing one customer that would produce a financial reward for me at that time of $2,000 to $10,000. This financial reward motivated me to keep calling until someone said "Yes!" By focusing on the reward, I was able to confidently move into action and destroy the wall of FUD that was keeping me from success. Those early days of cold calling were not very easy. However, by focusing on the rewards, I was able to overcome my fear of cold calling and actually got to a place where the rewards for my efforts were so good that I started looking forward to the days I made cold calls!

Destroy the Wall of Fear by Taking
Action So You Can Achieve Your Dreams

CONFIDENCE COACHING SOLUTION

Rewards motivate us to action.

The reward of a paycheck coming to you on Friday motivates you to get out of bed on a cold Monday morning and go to work. Even a stubborn, lazy donkey is motivated to action when you place a carrot in front of its face. Many people go through life and never get to experience the joy of actually eating the carrot. The only way I can stop a really hungry donkey that sees a carrot in front of his nose from moving to action so he can eat the carrot is to break his focus. If I can get the donkey to focus on the vomit that he threw up the last time he ate a carrot, it could cause the donkey to stop moving toward experiencing the same reward of eating the carrot.

> *I believe that life is constantly testing us for our level of commitment, and life's greatest rewards are reserved for those who demonstrate a never-ending commitment to act until they achieve.*
>
> —Anthony Robbins

Many people focus on their fears instead of focusing on the rewards that they will receive by destroying their fears with their corresponding action. Many people stop short of receiving their rewards in life because they allow their focus to be broken. There is nothing more discouraging and draining in life than to work hard and receive little or no reward for our effort. Now is the time to start moving toward the rewards you desire.

When is the best time to get started? *Right now!* This very minute! Start now before you take another step, waste another dollar, lose another sale, make another bad decision, work too many long and hard hours, or miss another important family event. Get the FUD out of your brain and prepare yourself for the next step of outrageous action coming from outrageous confidence, which will produce outrageous success!

America's Confidence Coach Reminds You . . .

- Action makes the difference between pretenders and contenders.
- Rewards motivate us to action.
- Outrageous confidence ignites outrageous actions, which produce outrageous rewards in life and business.
- Whoever acts more during the day, becomes more, does more, has more, and can help more.
- Uncommon acts create an uncommon confidence.
- When you say "I can do it," your fears go away and your self-confidence increases.

CONFIDENCE MAKEOVER STEPS NOW!

Answer the following questions:

1. What FUD are restraining you?
2. What lies are you telling yourself that need to cease?
3. What outrageous actions must you take to move toward your purpose, dreams, and success?
4. What timeline will you follow to get the FUD out of your life?
5. When you take action to obtain what you really want, what rewards will you receive?

Chapter 5

THE CONFIDENCE TO CHANGE

∽

WHEN I was eight years of age, my mother and father sat my brother and me down in our living room and informed us that they were getting divorced. I couldn't believe it. My thoughts raced and I asked myself over and over again, *Why?* My dad was a successful home builder in our area. I remember him always dressing in business suits and looking clean shaven. When my parents told me they were getting a divorce, two more thoughts entered my mind: *I must have done something wrong* and *My dad doesn't love me anymore.*

Six months later, my mom brought a man to our house to introduce him to my brother and me. Though dinner was a favorite of mine, spaghetti, I remember feeling really uncomfortable about this guy. Consequently, I was not hungry and could not eat. At the table, the man insisted I eat everything on my plate and when I didn't finish my food, he dumped the plate of spaghetti on top of my head. I felt worthless, humiliated, and hurt. After the incident, I cleaned up and I went to my bedroom and Mom came into my room to say goodnight. Then she told me she was getting married to this man in a few weeks.

For the next few years of my life, I lived in one of the most toxic environments for building a healthy level of confidence. My feelings as a boy about this man were right. My mother's new husband turned out to be an alcoholic, drug addict, and womanizer. I remember nights when he was in drunken rages and would beat my mother and try to pick fights with my brother and me. Any verbal expression about personal feelings was met with a slap across the face. One of the deep belief systems established in my subconscious was "It's wrong to express yourself!"

My real dad abandoned us for almost two years. I will never forget the first day I saw him again; he came to visit me after I broke my leg in a bicycle accident. He walked into my hospital room, and I was actually scared. I literally did not know who he was. Why? He had become a biker. He was an official member of the most dangerous motorcycle club in Fort Wayne, Satan's Escorts. His hair was long and I could hardly see his face because it was covered by a thick, long beard. I must say this blew me away because I only knew my father as a businessperson before he left us.

My new Satan's Escorts father introduced me to smoking marijuana at the tender age of thirteen and helped me with a contact so I could start selling drugs at sixteen. I was a party animal. I liked how alcohol gave me the confidence to ask girls to dance. I liked how marijuana made me feel happy for a couple of hours and caused me to forget the pressures of the present and the pain of the past.

I loved to go to bars and get really drunk so I could start fights and beat people up—that way I could release the anger I had deep inside toward my stepfather who physically and mentally abused my mother, my brother, and me. I had so much rage inside that I would sometimes fight three or four people at a time—and win.

My life was spinning out of control. I was hurting. I hated myself. I hated life. I hated people. My life was going nowhere.

The Defining Moment

In June 1990, after twenty-three years, I made a decision that changed the course of my life. The guilt and shame of the horrible life I was living was overwhelming me. I felt so dirty inside. I was so angry at everyone. Reinventing one's life starts in the moment of decision. I asked God that day to help me change my life so I could become the person I was destined to be. A radical change took place inside me as I received forgiveness from God. I forgave myself, forgave my parents, and forgave all those who had ever wronged me.

My childhood thoughts—*I'm stupid, I'm a bad person, I'm not good enough, I'm not loved, and it's wrong to express myself*—

had contaminated my adult life and were crippling me by hindering my confidence, true potential, and success.

Change is a door that can only be opened from the inside!
—Gary Eby

One of the most self-depreciating moments in my life was when I was twenty-four years old and sought out the advice of a pastor. I told him about my vision of speaking to thousands of people as an encourager and motivator for them. He looked me in the eye and said coldly, "God doesn't use people like you."

On the other hand, one of my greatest moments, and one that I treasure, came when I attended my twenty-year class reunion and our class president said I was voted the "most changed" person in our class. I used to be so embarrassed that I had been such a deadbeat. When people would ask me about my past, I would quickly change the subject. But now I realize that I am a shining example—if I can change, anybody can change.

The Emergency Brake That Inhibits Change

Audre Lorde said, "Revolution is not a one-time event." Applied to your life, this suggests that you are an ever-evolving, progressive work. So continue to develop yourself. Periodically, you must reinvent yourself. When things change and you don't, you become irrelevant. Change is the only constant in life. Examine your life and see what needs to be changed.

During your self-examination, expose and remove the obstacles to change and progress in your life. What are they? Here's a short list:

1. Learned Hopelessness—My life will never make a difference.

Learned hopelessness is a destructive belief system that says "No matter what action I take, nothing is going to change. I have tried and failed in the past, so nothing I do is going to make any difference. The world, people, and life are against me, and I can do nothing about it." When you feel like you have no control over your life, hopelessness and stress become your daily dancing partners, and confidence refuses to participate in the dance.

Learned hopelessness creates a "victim mentality." A victim viewpoint believes that people and circumstances are against you—that you have been exploited, taken advantage of, and are not in control. This belief system causes a person to become passive instead of aggressive, weak instead of strong, and pitiful instead of powerful. It causes a person to be consumed with focusing on problems and obstacles instead of solutions and possibilities.

A person becomes the victim of circumstances instead of the creator of his or her future. When you feel like you can do nothing about making your life better, that you are always being taken advantage of, abused, and put down, you are seeing yourself as a hopeless victim.

When you are victimized, you tend to focus on all the wrong another person has done to you. This flow of thinking is very self-destructive. Your focus is on the past and can cause you to turn into a very unhappy, mean, and bitter person.

What if you started looking at all these instances as *learning experiences*? Why not look at these negative experiences in a positive light—you have learned something from these experiences that has value. This thinking process moves you away from hopelessness or a victim's mentality to a victor's mind-set.

2. *Satisfaction and Contentment*—I can change anytime I want; now isn't a good time.

You have no sense of urgency! Your hunger and desire to change wane.

There once was a man who was seeking a clairvoyant to give him a reading of his future. When he found one, she told him, "I see many things about your future."

Excitedly, he asks, "Oh? Tell me what it looks like."

"Well," she says, "I see you as a poor and unhappy man up until the age of forty-five."

Feeling defeated, he dares himself to ask her, "What happens when I reach forty-five?"

"You get used to it," she says.

Accepting where you are gets you nowhere. Your future cannot be determined by your past. Being comfortable in your past keeps your present and future stale and uneventful. No progress will be made. Discontentment can motivate you to change.

3. *Playing the Blame Game*—Surely, I'm not to blame; you are!

Confident people take 100 percent responsibility for their lives. Insecure people refuse to take responsibility, so they play the blame game. I define blame as simply trying to give your problems to somebody or something else.

Blaming others renders you powerless. When you pass the blame on to somebody else, you rob yourself of your creative genius to solve your immediate problem.

"Blame, justification, and complaining are like pills. They are nothing more than stress reducers. They alleviate the stress of failure. Think about it."[1] Victims blame the economy; they blame the government, the stock market, their broker, their type of business, their employer, their employees, their manager, the head of their office, their up-line or their down-line, customer service, the shipping department, their partner, their spouse; they blame God, and, of course, they always blame their parents.

1 "Beginning Quotes," Brainy Quote, http://www.brainyquote.com/quotes/keywords/beginning_2.html.

4. *Throwing Change into the Future*—Someday I'm gonna . . . wait until . . . I should . . .

No one will ever water down your dreams as well as you do! For those who are satisfied to walk in mediocrity, the highway of life has always been paved with good intentions. "Someday I'm gonna . . ." become the empty words of people who refuse to grasp the moments that are before them.

5. *Denial and Self-deception*—This isn't really happening to me.

I call this the "it's not me" syndrome. This belief system will not allow people to see negative realities about themselves. They can see issues in everybody else's lives but not in their own personal lives. However, like a driver with blinders on, they cannot see that they have the same issues and their behaviors are driving them into disaster. Something internally keeps them from facing the facts preventing them from making the necessary changes that will help them reinvent their lives and organizations.

I have heard these people talk negatively about other people and I think, *Gee, you do the exact same thing in your own life.*

I have had leaders and coaching clients over the years suddenly cut off all contact with me. Some of them completely disappeared from my life. I often wondered, *What happened to these people? I really wanted to help them.* Then after several years, many resurface. "What happened you? We were making such good progress and then you quit," I ask.

Here is the reply I have received time and time again: "Keith Johnson, you were forcing me to face the hard truths about myself that I did not want to deal with, so I stopped liking you and the coaching process. Now I realize that all you were doing was trying to help me become better. Now I'm ready! Can you help me?"

Denial is a defense mechanism that shields us from painful thoughts. Facing the truth about the outcomes in our lives is not always easy. As a matter of fact, it can be quite painful. Denial is an internal thinking process that people use to remove responsibility from themselves and place it on someone or something else.

Deniers stick their heads in the sand and pretend nothing is wrong.

1. I don't want to face the truth.
2. Anybody who makes me face the truth is my enemy.
3. I don't think I need to change.
4. I have my act together.
5. I don't really want to change because my behavior is helping me meet my needs.

6. *Replacement*—I'll live my life through helping you.

The greatest help you can be to somebody else is to show them how you have been able to change your own life for the better. I often say, "The best thing you can do for the poor is not be one of them." Confident people admit the reality that they have problems, face their own problems, and deal with them. Insecure people ignore their own problems, focus on other people's problems, and never deal with their own issues. They focus on everybody else's problems and issues so the spotlight does not have to shine on their own.

Do you know anybody whose own life is really messed up but they are always trying to help others? These people are emotionally confused. Instead of dealing with their own issues, they become what I call a Dr. Phil to everybody else. They know what everybody else needs to do to change their lives. They notice everybody's problems and have all the cures. I have seen some of these people try to help others fix their lives, which keeps them from looking at their own lives. Instead of living their own lives, they live vicariously through someone else who is in worse shape. They often act like they do not like all the drama in other people's lives, but in actuality, they feed off it because it makes them feel important.

7. *The Sorry Man*—I'm sorry for my bad behavior, but I can't change it.

I witnessed this firsthand while I was being raised. My mother's new husband would stay out all night at the bars getting drunk, chasing women, and spending all the money he earned on partying instead of paying the bills and buying groceries. Of course, when he got caught and my mother would threaten him with divorce, which was about every month, he would come back home with "presents" for my mother and for us. He would cry and tell my mother how sorry he was and that he would never do it again. He would promise us he was going to stop drinking and treating us badly. You can probably guess how the story goes. Yes, my mother would feel sorry for him because he had no place to stay; and after all, he was upset and crying so he must be really serious this time. And guess what, he would stop drinking and start treating her nicely for a while until he was back into the house. But his so-called changed behavior would be short-lived.

As a child and now a man, I have seen this story played out over and over again, not only in my mother's life but also in many of my clients' lives.

There is a difference between being sorry for your behavior and reinventing yourself. Reinvention requires a true turnaround. It requires what the Bible calls repentance. When people repent, they make the decision to never turn back to the old, destructive patterns of behavior. These people have a clear understanding of how their behavior hurts them as well as the people around them, and they do not want this to happen anymore.

I have found that being *sorry* is a feeling generated by getting caught, while *repentance* for transformation comes from the inside of people who have a hunger to change who they are.

8. *The Story You Keep Telling Yourself*—This just keeps happening over and over again.

Of all the emergency brakes, this one is the most common. What is really stopping you from going from where you are to where you want to be? It is your story. Yes! Your story. You see, EVERYBODY HAS A STORY. The story is the REASON why you cannot succeed.

- Why you cannot change your circumstances.
- Why you cannot make the changes in your company that are long overdue.
- Why you cannot get the job you always longed for.
- Why you cannot make the money you really want and deserve.
- Why you cannot go to college and get more education.
- Why you cannot have outrageous success in life.

What is the story you keep telling yourself over and over again like a broken record?

Here are a few common stories I have helped clients erase from their minds over the years:

"I don't have enough money."

"I don't have enough education."

"I tried everything and nothing works."

"I cannot make great money because I live in a certain geographical spot."

"I don't have time."

"My divorce totally ruined my reputation and my checkbook."

"I don't have the right color of skin. If I were born _____ (white, black, brown, etc.), I could succeed."

"My family was raised poor so I guess I will be poor also."

"People who are successful and rich are all crooked,
    so I don't want to be like them."
"Nobody wants to help me."

So what is the story you keep playing in your mind over and over again?

You have a story about why you cannot experience outrageous success in life. You have a story about why you cannot change. You have a story about why you cannot grow your business.

Everybody has a story about why they can't. . . . They replay this story every time the opportunity to change presents itself.

9. *The Ultimate Lie*—I have tried everything!

I have a friend who moved to America to live the American Dream. He wanted to be a speaker and coach like I am. I gave him a list of twenty-five immediate action steps that he needed to take to be successful. However, his wife told me he only did one or two of them and simply quit. My friend finally decided he was going to go back to his country where it was "easier" to succeed. On the day of his departure, he looked into my eyes and said, "Keith, I don't want to leave this country, but you know I have tried everything I know to succeed and nothing has worked. Don't you agree?"

I gracefully looked him square in the eyes and put on my

coaching hat, and instead of giving him a direct answer, I asked him, "You tried EVERYTHING?"

He quickly replied, "Yes! I have tried everything!"

I said, "Really? Name everything you tried one by one. Start by naming at least five of the twenty-five action steps I told you to do to build your speaking business that you actually applied."

He slowly named off a total of three and proceeded to give me all the negative "stories" about why each of them did not work for him. One hour later, three long stories later, I discovered that he had tried only three action steps. Then he quickly changed the subject and invited me to visit him in his country in the future.

One time I was coaching a motivational speaker who taught some great information; but in order to go to the next level, he needed to write the information in a book. His story? "I don't have enough time to write a book." I said, "Oh? How much time do you spend every day watching television, surfing the Internet, or playing video games? You have enough time . . . this is just the story you keep telling yourself."

The Triangle of Change and Reinvention

When change is a "must," your mind will find a way to make it happen. When change is a "should," you only attempt change when you feel it will hurt less and you will be most comfortable. Procrastination will stymie your change.

CONFIDENCE COACHING SOLUTION

Make change a MUST!

1. I MUST MAKE CHANGES NOW!

I must change now! I found that all successful people I've ever spoken to had a turning point. The turning point was when they made a clear, specific, unequivocal decision that they were not going to continue living a certain way; they were going to achieve success. Some people make that decision at age fifteen and some people make it at fifty; most people never make it at all.

The key word is NOW! In order to bring about the changes that are necessary in your life or organization, you must create a sense of URGENCY. Complacency is the enemy of transformation.

Many people say, "I have tried to make changes before and they did not work, so I'm afraid to try again even though I know I need to make the change." The biggest mistake I see when I am consulting with people, especially leaders, is that they try to make changes without creating a sense of urgency and an understanding within the organization—"if we do not change, we will not have jobs in the future." As a matter of fact, I tell leaders to use the current crisis as a launching pad to bring about the changes they need. Crisis comes on the curve of change. Many times leaders overestimate how much change they can bring about, and they underestimate how difficult it can be to get people out of their conditioned patterns and comfort zones.

2. I BELIEVE CHANGE IS POSSIBLE.

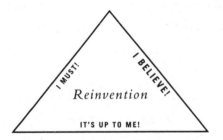

You can associate change with pleasure instead of pain. Your self-talk is *I believe change is possible*. Whatever you truly believe, with passion, becomes your future reality. Your behaviors will constantly be in harmony with your belief systems, especially the belief systems about yourself.

You do not necessarily believe what you see; you believe what you already have seen. The filters in your mind will automatically reject anything that is contrary to what you really believe at a subconscious level.

Can you actually see the changes you want to make in your life? Can you see yourself making the income you have always desired? Can you see your business? Can you see yourself becoming the top salesperson at your company? Can you see yourself married to the person of your dreams?

Really, can you close your eyes and see it?

I believe change is possible. What is seeable is believable. What is believable is possible. I asked one client to close his eyes and tell me what he saw himself becoming in the future. He opened his eyes and said, "Nothing." So what was he getting out of life? Nothing. He was at the critical stage in which he needed to implement the reinvention triangle in his life.

How did I help this client change his life, explode his business, and skyrocket his income? I helped him believe that change was possible. I challenged him to overcome his limited belief system, like I am challenging you, and to engage his imagination and see his bright new future being realized. What is visible becomes believable. What is believable becomes possible. What is possible, once acted on, becomes reality.

Self-limiting beliefs derail your progress. These beliefs exist when you start believing the lie that you are prevented from changing your life, achieving a goal, or getting something you always wanted.

As I shared earlier, my limiting beliefs started in childhood with such thoughts as *I'm stupid, I'm a bad person, I'm not good enough, I'm not loved,* and *it's wrong to express myself.* These self-limiting beliefs had contaminated my adult life and were crippling me by hindering my confidence, true potential, and success.

Self-limiting beliefs act like brakes on your potential. They hold you back. They stop you from acceleration. They create fear, uncertainty, and doubt. They paralyze you and cause you to hesitate to take the risks that are necessary for you to achieve your dreams. They slow down your progress. They keep you from reinventing yourself.

In order for you to reinvent yourself, to progress, to move forward, to skyrocket your income, and to go upward in your life and business, you must continually challenge your belief systems. You must reject any thought that says you are limited in any way. You must accept that there are NO LIMITS over your life, only those you put on yourself.

If other people have achieved something, you can achieve it too. Free your mind from FUD! Imagine you have no limitations to who you can become, what you can do, the amount of income you can earn, and the number of people you can help!

Understand that the FUD person seeks financial security in staying where they are and hoarding what they have, believing that losing everything is possible and risk is untenable. But the person with a Confidence Solution reaches and seeks financial increase and will create an abundance of wealth with multiple streams of income.

The FUD person believes that total security rests in one income source or a JOB (Just Over Broke), while the person reinventing herself or himself will create multiple streams of income so that if one declines, then another stream increases so that wealth continues to grow.

You must believe with all your heart that changing your life, career, business, and income is possible!

3. CHANGE IS UP TO ME!

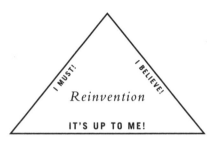

Reinventing your life or organization is up to you. The big question: Are you going to lead your life and organization or are you going to just manage the status quo? Leaders look into the future and see the divine possibilities then come back into the present and make the necessary changes so they can produce a future reality.

Successful people take responsibility for changing their personal and professional lives. Taking responsibility for change means:

- You must stop blaming everybody else for your outcomes.
- You must become dissatisfied with your current results.
- Eliminate the stories you keep telling yourself about why this change cannot happen.

- You must stop waiting for outside circumstances to change.
- You must stop waiting for other people to change.
- You must stop waiting on God to change it when He wants you to do it.
- You must stop throwing change into the future and make it happen today.

Begin the process of change through reinventing yourself, exploding your business, and skyrocketing your income by telling yourself the truth about yourself, your present situation, and your past. That truth will set you free from the "emergency brakes" of your past and allow you to use pain and pleasure as a lever. Remember . . .

Too often times it happens that we live our lives in chains and we never realize we have the keys.
> —Eagles' song "I Am Already Gone"

Everyone thinks of changing the world, but no one thinks of changing himself.
> —Leo Tolstoy

Leveraging the Power of Reinvention

You can leverage your pain and pleasure to affect change in your life. How does that work?

❀ Pain = My history will repeat itself if I do not change.

❀ Pleasure = My future will be better than my past.

Pain can destroy you or drive you.

We are all motivated to actions that increase pleasure and reduce pain. Procrastination arises from the fear of the increased pain that would result from taking action instead of maintaining the status quo. We must move beyond procrastination. "Waiting to see what happens" simply leads to more pain.

A toothache is a classic case in point. Many people will put off a trip to the dentist indefinitely—that is until they reach a maximum pain threshold. They don't act until they experience an intensity of pain or discomfort that compels them to create change. In the end, the prospect of an extraction seems less painful than the chronic throbbing of an aching tooth. After enough pain, the dentist has become the lesser of two evils.

At this point, however, pain has become our ally. It is a powerful assistant in providing the leverage we need to create positive change. In order to change, you must ask yourself these questions:

Pain-inducing Questions
  ❀ *What will it cost if I don't master this area of my life?*
  ❀ *What will happen if I don't turn things around?*
  ❀ *What is the price I will pay?*
  ❀ *What will I miss out on?*
  ❀ *What will I fail to achieve?*
  ❀ *Whom will I hurt?*

Once you have truthfully answered these questions, then allow *pleasure* to motivate your change. Ask yourself:

Pleasure-inducing Questions
- ❀ *How will my life be greater if I truly master this area of my life now?*
- ❀ *How will my energy, happiness, joy, or success explode?*
- ❀ *What will I gain?*
- ❀ *Whom can I help?*
- ❀ *What will I achieve?*

To go to the next level, you must create a larger capacity for confidence in order to handle the increasing level of pressure, the stress from increasing responsibility, and the chaos that progress produces. Every change produces a new level of pain. Be proactive by increasing your Confidence Solution to handle it.

Use pain and pleasure to spur you to change and reinvent yourself. Remember, change isn't a preference, it's a conviction—a must! Once change becomes a necessity in your life, you are now ready to move into the Triangle of Confidence.

America's Confidence Coach Reminds You . . .

- See yourself as life's student, not life's victim.
- Now is the best time to start changing.

- You must stop blaming others for your problems and inability to change.
- Stop procrastinating.
- Tell yourself the truth.
- Live your own life, not someone else's.
- Stop telling yourself the same old stories over and over again.
- Make change a MUST!

CONFIDENCE MAKEOVER STEPS NOW!

As you change, ask yourself:

1. How have I been changing on the inside lately?
2. How have I changed in the last week?
3. How have I changed in the last month?
4. How have I changed in the last year?
5. What will it cost me if I don't change?
6. What will I miss out on in my life if I don't change now?
7. If I do change, how will it make me feel about myself?
8. What kind of momentum will I create if I make this change right now?
9. What can I achieve if I make this change?
10. How much happier will I be if I start changing right now?

Chapter 6

THE CONFIDENCE OF SELF

If there is one quality you could have that would make you successful in motivating people or convincing people to follow your lead, that trait would be
CONFIDENCE.

—DR. JOHN MAXWELL

∞

How do you see yourself? When you look into the mirror, what do you see? This is a very important question; you should really take a moment and think about it.

The word *image* is the root word of imagination, meaning something in the mind. Your self-image is simply a mental picture of how you see yourself. Developing a positive self-image is based on the principle that each of us is the product of what we think, perceive, and believe about ourselves. The more positive your self-image, the more opportunities you will have to achieve success. Eventually, all of us have to come to grips with how we see ourselves.

Your self-image determines how you see yourself, the world, and life in general. How you see yourself determines how you will function in life. You must have a visual photograph of what you want to become, achieve, or possess in your future. Why? Because you are motivated to become what you picture yourself to be.

CONFIDENCE COACHING SOLUTION

*You are motivated to become what you
picture yourself to be.*

Your behavior is a mirror image revealing your self-portrait. If you see yourself as a champion in life, you will be motivated to develop all the positive qualities and actions of a winner. However, if you see yourself as a loser, you will continue to experience one failure after another in life.

If you see yourself as being ignorant, you will always have difficulty with your ability to study, read, and learn new facts. Then you will develop an attitude of "I have a hard time reading and studying." Therefore, you will not even try.

If you see yourself as being poor, you will continue to live in poverty. If you see yourself as a klutz in sports, you will fumble all over yourself on the court. If you see yourself as a poor communicator, you will always have a hard time developing relationships with other people or speaking in front of crowds. The more you tell yourself that you are ugly, hopeless, worthless, a failure, or unable to do something, the more deeply embedded that self-image becomes.

Next is the Confidence Triangle, which includes three important dynamics: self-image, self-esteem, and self-talk. I will unpack each one of these for you and explain how they interface to build your confidence.

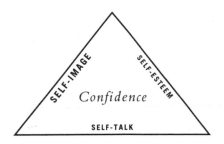

Point 1— Self-Image Forms the Foundation for Confidence

When changing your self-image into a positive, motivating dynamic, you must consider three essential facts:

Fact 1. You will only rise to the level of your own self-image.

Your self-image is like a thermostat that will only allow you to perform within the prescribed range. You will act and perform in direct response to your self-image. It is axiomatic that "water always seeks its own level." You will always live your life at the level of your self-image.

When fishing, the angler throws his line into the water and the bobber will naturally rise to the level of the water.

Once the bobber rises all the way to the top of the water, it hits a "glass ceiling" that keeps it from going any higher than the water level of the lake. In the same way, your low self-image creates an invisible glass ceiling over you, preventing you from achieving your full potential.

CONFIDENCE COACHING SOLUTION

You can never outperform your inner self-image.

The first step toward improving your job performance has nothing to do with the job itself but instead with improving how you feel about yourself. People will rapidly rise in life, business, performance, or success in relation to the level of their self-image.

Once that level is reached, you stop the progress of your full potential. A *positive* self-image enables you to set goals for your future that will reflect your true potential. A distorted photograph of yourself, created by your *negative* belief systems, will create a glass ceiling that limits you from achieving higher levels of success in life.

Images are created in all of us by the words we hear and the pictures we see. We are told that two-thirds of our lifetime impressions are made before we are seven years old. In reality, your self-image was formed in your mind during your childhood. In order for you to change the wrong image you have of yourself, you must first change the way you think about yourself.

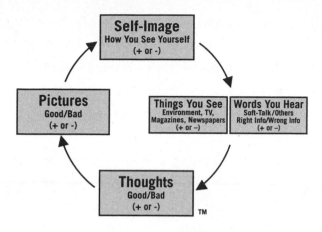

Your thoughts are a product of the words you hear (self-talk and others) and the pictures (environment, television, magazines, newspapers) you see. Thoughts create images in your mind. The words that you hear create the thoughts that generate the pictures in your mind. If I said "pink elephant," your mind would instantly picture a pink elephant.

Changing the place from where you get your information can erase negative thoughts and pictures. Delete the negative thoughts and images that your parents may have spoken around you, what your ex-spouse said about you, what doctors might have told you, or what your old schoolmates used to say about you. This is wrong information that must be rejected so you can create a new self-image.

Start thinking new thoughts, and you will begin to see a new picture of yourself. What you start picturing in your mind you will begin to accomplish. When you change your picture, you automatically change your performance.

Fact 2. You can delete your old self-image.

One of the most powerful things you can do in life is to create a new, positive self-image. The next most powerful thing you can do is to destroy all negative images you have of yourself.

The picture you have of yourself has been developed in the darkroom of your past experiences. Each failure, success, and the way your parents raised you created either positive or negative images of yourself.

I recently purchased a new digital camera. I love my camera because after every shot I take, I can review it. I can choose to delete the distorted or ugly pictures. I can also choose to keep all the good pictures. You can choose to delete the digital photographs in your mind and take a new snapshot of the successful, confident, new you.

Fact 3. You can create a new image of success.

The "you" you see today is nothing compared to the "you" you can become! Developing a new picture of yourself is the way to move into a new realm of success in life. Stop looking at the ugly, distorted picture of yourself. Stop seeing yourself through your failure glasses. Go buy a set of success glasses. See yourself as a confident champion in life, full of potential, enthusiasm, personality, and promise.

Discover Your Self-Concept

Your self-concept centers on the adjectives you use to define yourself. Fill in the blanks with words that come to mind when you think about yourself. For example, I am optimistic/pessimistic, productive/lazy, etc.

I am _____.

When you have more negative adjectives than positive ones, you have a negative self-concept. The key to personal growth is to change the negatives into positives and then you will project a positive image to others.

How you see yourself is more important than how others see you.

Top ten most common negative "I am" messages:

1. I am worthless.
2. I am fat.
3. I am poor.
4. I am ugly.
5. I am a failure.
6. I am stupid.
7. I am a misfit.
8. I am bad.
9. I am an accident.
10. I am unloved.

How many of these negative statements do you make about yourself?

Now, let's look at the positive "I am" statements that you need to make about yourself.

1. I am worthy of success, happiness, and peace of mind.
2. I am loved, accepted, and valuable.
3. I am brilliant and beautiful.
4. I am smart enough to do anything I want.
5. I am smart enough to figure out a solution to my problem.
6. I am good enough.
7. I am unique.
8. I am a person of destiny.
9. I am capable.
10. I am filled with abundant gifts and talents.

Never Allow Others to Determine Your Self-Image

Do not allow other people to create in you an image of failure or destroy your image of success. In order for you to live at your full potential and fulfill your destiny in life, you have got to get out of the box that people like to put you in and the box that you may put yourself in.

Stop believing what other people have said about you and your future. Refuse to allow other people to destroy your confidence. Look at yourself in the mirror and see yourself as strong, confident, intelligent, successful, and good-looking: a true champion in life.

Point 2—You Need Self-Esteem

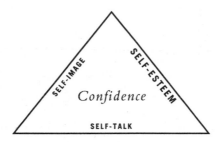

What is self-esteem? Self-esteem is how much you love or like yourself. It is your own personal estimation of your worth to the world. It is the value that you place upon who you are and what you do. Your self-esteem, in turn, is determined by your self-image, which we have just discovered.

Jesus taught that the greatest commandment was to love God with all one's heart, mind, and strength. He further taught that the second commandment was to love one's neighbor as one's self. In other words, loving ourselves isn't a matter of arrogant pride; it's the right thing to do. Loving self builds self-esteem.

Dr. Nathaniel Branden is known as the psychologist who awakened America's consciousness to the importance of self-esteem. He made this profound statement in his book *How to Raise Your Self-Esteem*:

Apart from problems that are biological in origin, I cannot think of a single psychological difficulty—from anxiety and depression, to fear of intimacy or of success, to alcohol or drug abuse, to underachievement at school or at work, to spouse battering or child molestation, to sexual dysfunctions or emotional immaturity, to suicide or crimes of violence—that is not traceable to poor self-esteem. Of all the judgments we pass, none is as important as the one we pass on ourselves. Positive self-esteem is a cardinal requirement of a fulfilling life.[1]

You are valuable. Some estimate that the worth of just your physical being is millions of dollars.

Following is another opinion from the Indiana University School of Medicine:

How much is a human body worth? When broken down into fluids, tissues, and germ fighting, our bodies are worth more than $45 million.

This price tag on the human body is based on a survey published in Wired *magazine. It found that vital organs are no longer the most valuable body parts. Rather, bone marrow heads the list . . . priced at $23 million, based on 1,000 grams*

---

1 Nathaniel Branden, *How to Raise Your Self-Esteem* (New York: Bantam Doubleday Dell, 1987), p. 5.

at $23,000 per gram. DNA can fetch $9.7 million, while extracting antibodies can bring $7.3 million. A lung is worth $116,400, a kidney $91,400, and a heart $57,000.

Women's eggs are costlier than men's sperm. The survey found that a fertile woman could sell thirty-two egg cells over eight years for $224,000; however, for a man to earn the same amount, he would have to make twelve sperm donations a month for twenty years.

The prices are based on cost estimates taken from hospitals and insurance companies, and are based on projected prices only in the United States. Of course, the prices also assume that all these substances can be extracted from living tissue for sale.[2]

Others will not value you unless you value yourself. In fact, your self-esteem projects your worth to others. If I believe I am worthless, others will pick up on that nonverbal message and begin to treat me as worthless. Positive self-esteem projects confidence.

I once asked a client to tell me what my consulting time was worth to him. That person answered my question with a question, "What are you worth?" He had no idea what my experience, knowledge, education, skills, and talents were worth. He had to rely on how I valued myself. I charged what I felt I was worth, and he paid that without question. Don't

2 "You Are Worth $45,000,000.00!" International Suicide Prevention, http://www.supportisp.org/How_much_am_I_worth.htm.

sell yourself short! You must first skyrocket your personal value before you will ever skyrocket your personal income.

Discover your value. Improving your self-esteem starts by changing the way you think about the value of each human being on this earth—especially yourself! You are unique, one of a kind. You are worth millions of dollars!

There is nobody in the world like you. Nobody else in this world has the exact same voice as you. Nobody has the same fingerprint or DNA as you. Nobody has the same facial features or expressions you do. This makes you special. Therefore, you have something you can contribute to the world that nobody else can give.[3]

Now life's experiences may wear us down. People may attack, criticize, or demean us. But we choose whether we allow circumstances to tear away at our self-esteem or allow our inner courage and confidence to shape our mental self-portrait.

Try this exercise. From the following two lists, circle the words that best describe who you are:

Intelligent	*Dumb*
Discerning	*Insensitive*
Adaptive	*Rigid*

3 John E. Gibson, "Purpose and Passion—What Makes the Difference Between Success and Failure?" *Success,* September 1977.

Inventive	*Uncreative*
Resourceful	*Inadequate*
Persistent	*Easily distracted*
Patient	*Impatient*
Curious	*Disinterested*
Energetic	*Lazy*
Fun-loving	*Sad*
Humorous	*Boring*
Dynamic	*Powerless*
Attractive	*Homely*
Generous	*Stingy*
Respectful	*Critical*
Confident	*Insecure*

If you circled more adjectives in the right-hand column than the left, your self-esteem is suffering and needs rebuilding and reviving. It's time to create a mental picture of yourself that is colored by your strengths, not contaminated by your weaknesses.

Continually remind yourself that a failed enterprise doesn't make you a failure. Thomas Edison failed thousands of times trying to find the right filament for the lightbulb. He confidently persisted until he succeeded. Motivational speaker Zig Ziglar often says, "Failure is not a person; it's an event."

When you fail, what do you tell yourself? How do you talk to yourself? Do you focus on what you have learned and what not to do next time, or do you berate and belittle yourself?

Your self-talk can make or break your confidence. Positive self-esteem gives you the confidence you need to encourage yourself when circumstances and other people discourage you. It's time to take your confident self-esteem and talk yourself into confidence.

Point 3—Self-Talk Yourself into Confidence

The third point on the Confidence Triangle is self-talk. Throughout the day you are continually talking to yourself. What you say can make you feel confident or insecure, fearful or courageous, good or bad. Zig Ziglar says that 77 percent of all people practice negative self-talk.

Have you ever been around a person who always talks about how many aches and pains they have in their body? How about someone who always talks bad about themselves? Their self-talk is centered on how "bad" they are or how "bad" they feel.

Therefore, they actually feel bad. And as surprising as it may seem, almost 77 percent of all sickness is psychosomatic.

If what you say can make you feel bad, then what you say can also make you feel confident on a daily basis. What *you* are saying about you, your talents, your abilities, your personal worth, and your future is more important than what others are saying about you.

Self-Talk Is Self-Coaching

Develop the art of self-coaching. Ask yourself questions and listen to the answers. Pay attention to your internal dialogue.

I have a client who talks so much that he never listens to anything anybody else is saying to him, including his wife, his customers, and me, his coach. His lack of listening over the years caused him to miss applying the confidence keys I recommended. After he makes a mistake, he says, "Why didn't you warn me?" My response: "I told you, but apparently you weren't listening."

Much of our inner dialogue is so deeply imbedded into our subconscious that we don't even realize consciously what we are telling our inner selves.

Embrace a Totally Affirming Lifestyle

What is a totally affirming lifestyle? It's when you start living a "judge not" lifestyle and stop living a "judge everything" lifestyle. Putting yourself down, judging yourself, or being hard on yourself tears at your self-esteem.

Many people with low self-esteem live in a perpetual cycle of judgmental lifestyle. Release all kinds of judgments about yourself and others. While you cannot change your personal history, you can remove the negative self-judgments and negative belief systems you have created about yourself. Resetting your mind-set requires you to first reconcile your negative past experiences and change your belief system.

I remember when I faced my mental health breakdown on March 16, 2002. All of the internal judgments I placed on myself came to the surface that day. I started saying what was held as a deep belief system at a subconscious level.

My thoughts in crisis that rose out of my judgmental, critical mind-set were:

- I'll never amount to anything.
- I'm a loser.
- I'm destined for failure so why even try.
- I'm an idiot.
- Who am I kidding? I will never accomplish these crazy dreams.
- I'm not worth anything, I should just kill myself.
- I should just go get a job at the car wash; at least I will not be disappointed.

Crisis often becomes the tool that reveals our subconscious thoughts and belief systems. It is like a mud puddle. When calm, the water looks clean. When stirred, all the mud at the bottom comes to the top. Crisis seasons do not create the pain. They create a trigger that reveals the thought patterns already existing in your subconscious. These value and thought patterns are the root cause of the negative outcomes you have been experiencing in life.

When I faced the worst day of my adult life, all these negative beliefs about myself surfaced. However, on a normal day I would not have had all those thoughts on a conscious level. My personal crisis caused me to see that beneath the surface, I had some internal beliefs that were paralyzing me—holding me back from achieving my true potential. My real belief systems were coming out in the midst of my personal crisis. The crisis became a tool that God used to reveal the unfinished business that I needed to deal with in order to increase my Confidence Thermostat setting.

Infirmed or Affirmed?

People are starved for affirmation today. When you are hungry, you are driven to do what is necessary to get what you want. When you are starved for affirmation, you are driven to perform in order to be affirmed. Sadly, some hungry people will eat anything, so they spend their lives trying to please people who *infirm* them instead of *affirm* them.

Consider this: *To be infirmed is to be made weak and feeble. To be affirmed is to be made strong and firm.*

Words are the seedbed of your feelings. Therefore your

words create an emotional punch that can make your emotional state either strong or weak based on the internal and external words (self-talk) you speak.

To boost your confidence, it is important that on a regular basis you receive affirming words from yourself and important people in your life. Hearing affirming words from your mentors, spouse, and parents helps boost your confidence, makes you strong, and, most important, brings healing to your soul.

Guard your soul against infirming words from yourself and others. Get in touch with your emotional feelings. They are your feelings and they have value. When somebody says something to you that devalues you, have the confidence to express your feeling by saying, "You know, when you say those things to me, it really bothers me emotionally. I would appreciate it if you stopped saying those things." This is how you "guard" your soul. If the person refuses to be considerate of your feelings, you may want to disconnect from that relationship or simply reduce the time you spend with that person.

America's Confidence Coach Reminds You . . .

- You are motivated to become what you picture yourself to be.
- You can never outperform your inner self-image.
- Your self-image is rooted in God.

- The goal of every enemy in your life is to destroy your self-portrait.
- How you see yourself determines the level of success you will achieve in life.
- Stop trying to be somebody or something you are not.
- You can make a difference and your difference can make you.
- Allow your difference to define you and not confine you.
- Champions know the secret of positive self-talk.

CONFIDENCE MAKEOVER STEPS NOW!

1. Identify the people in your life who *infirm* you. How many hours do you spend with them per week? What do you need to do to spend less time with these people?
2. Identify the people in your life that *affirm* you. How many hours per week do you spend with them? How can you increase time spent with these people?
3. Stop making negative, judgmental statements about yourself.
4. Make daily positive "I am" confessions.

Chapter 7

THE CONFIDENCE TO SUCCEED

Success is knowing my purpose, growing to my
maximum potential, and sowing seeds that benefit others.

—DR. JOHN MAXWELL

EVEN at a young age, I knew what I wanted. I wanted to be cool, I wanted people to like me (especially attractive girls), and I wanted to become wealthy like many of my childhood friends' dads.

I rejected spiritual stuff. I (maybe like you?) was approached by several different people from different religious backgrounds wanting me to be part of their "religious club." I did not want to become spiritual because I saw how these spiritual people lived and I did not want to be part of it. My personal perception of religious people was that they were all (1) broke (poor materially or relationally) and (2) nerds. I had great dreams and aspirations of being a wealthy businessman; I did not have time for spiritual stuff. The whole external dynamic always turned me off. The special clothing, the holy objects and spiritual giftware, and all the trappings of religion didn't appeal to me. Although I wanted to be spiritual, I did not want to be weird. I did not want to become broke or a nerd.

Who do you have when nobody else believes in your dream, business, or message? There are going to be times in your journey through life when your path is going to take you places that people will think are crazy. Yes! Even some of those people who are right beside you right now will think that. For me, in the midst of the negative voices and unsupportive people, knowing that God was on my side and wanted me to succeed caused my confidence levels to take a quantum leap. At the writing of this book, I have spread the message of confidence in eight different countries in one year. Suddenly, those who were not on board with me are congratulating me for my successes.

Both faith and confidence are needed if you are to have the personal power to achieve outrageous success in life through reinventing yourself. Faith is based in having trust in another's abilities. Confidence, on the other hand, is having a solid belief in yourself and in your own abilities. Having faith in God, a higher power, gives you the feeling of external power and strength to continue to pursue your dreams; having confidence in your abilities to achieve your dreams will give you the inner power to perform at your best in challenging situations.

It was a tragedy that sent shockwaves around the world. On October 25, 1999, a small plane plummeted to the ground near Mina, South Dakota, killing everyone aboard. Among them was golfing great Payne Stewart. Just a few months earlier, he had captured the U.S. Open in storybook fashion after a devastating loss in the same tournament the year before. He was back at the top of his game and brimming with confidence. But when he accepted the trophy, he surprised everyone by saying, "First of all, I have to give thanks to the Lord. If it weren't for the faith that I have in Him, I wouldn't have been able to have the faith that I had in myself on the golf course."[1] Confidence in God had instilled personal confidence. Really?

The most confident business entrepreneur I know is Donald Trump. Surely his confidence has nothing to do with God. Right? Listen to his own words from his book *Trump: Think Like a Billionaire:*

> *Some of you may think it's wrong to talk about God and business in the same breath, but God has always been central to our way of thinking about capitalism. The Protestant work ethic has thrived for centuries. The pursuit of prosperity is ingrained in our religious culture. The more you have, the more you can give.*
>
> *Here's something else about God that any billionaire knows: He's in the details, and you need to be there, too.*[2]

1 Tracey Stewart with Ken Abraham, *Payne Stewart* (Nashville: Broadman & Holman Publishers, 2000). Taken from a Good News Publishers handout, Wheaton, Illinois.

2 Donald J. Trump with Meredith McIver, *Trump: Think Like a Billionaire: Everything You Need to Know About Success, Real Estate, and Life* (New York: Ballentine Books, 2005), p. xii.

God wants you to skyrocket your income and become prosperous. So, God will be integral to that, as Trump implies.

God and faith, keys to confidence? How's that? When we start looking and listening for the word *confidence*, it's amazing how often the word is used in our daily vocabulary. Sports announcers use the word to describe an athlete's impressive performance. Businesses create television commercials that build the customer's confidence in their services or products. Motivational speakers and training coaches talk about the need for confidence. The financial markets report on and rely on investor confidence. Pastors use the word to encourage their parishioners.

Interestingly, "confidence" appears over one hundred times in different forms throughout the Christian Scriptures. One biblical commentator remarked, "Achievers are confident. They believe against all odds that they will win and succeed. We read that faith, hope, and love are a winning triad. Know the definition of hope: 'confident assurance!'"[3]

The Creator designed amazing creatures with supreme confidence. Do you know what the world's strongest living creature is? It's the horned dung beetle. In a laboratory experiment, Rob Knell from Queen Mary University of London and Leigh Simmons from the University of Western Australia found that the strongest *Onthophagus taurus* could pull 1,141

3 Mike Murdock, *One-Minute Pocket Bible for the Achiever* (Dallas: Wisdom International, 1994), p. iii.

times its own body weight. That's equivalent to a person lifting close to 180,000 pounds (the weight of six full double-decker buses).[4] How is this possible? Because the horned dung beetle never had outside voices telling it that lifting such a weight was impossible.

The biblical narrative reports that the first human being, Adam, was created with great confidence. Adam had a supreme level of self-confidence. When God brought all the animals before Adam to name, Adam did not doubt his ability to give each animal a specific name. What a huge challenge!

There are millions of different species of animals on the earth. Go ahead, try it yourself. Start naming some animals and see how many you can name. What caused Adam to accomplish such an incredible task? It was Adam's supreme level of confidence in his own abilities that empowered him to perform at his full potential. With outside voices (or inside voices) telling him that he could do it, a confident Adam *did it*!

If my guess is right, you have not been as fortunate as Adam or the beetle. *They* told you that your dream was too big, your abilities too common, and your finances too limited. What do *they* know? They didn't create you, and they don't know you! Don't you think that it is time for you to stop allowing those outside and inside voices to kill your dreams?

---

4 "Strongest Creature—Horned Dung Beetle," Extreme Science, http://www .extremescience.com/zoom/index.php/creepy-crawlies/117-strongest-animal.

CONFIDENCE COACHING SOLUTION

God + (You + Confidence) + Other People
= You Can Accomplish Anything.

Mother Teresa of Calcutta had a dream. She told her superiors, "I have three pennies and a dream from God to build an orphanage."

"Mother Teresa," her superiors chided gently, "you cannot build an orphanage with three pennies. With three pennies, you can't do anything!"

"I know," she said, smiling, "but with God and three pennies I can do anything!"[5]

Yes, with God's help and your effort, mixed with massive doses of confidence, you can accomplish anything you set your mind to do. The foundation of your confidence is built on what I call the Success Triangle.

5 Jack Canfield and Mark Victor Hansen, *The Aladdin Factor* (New York: Berkley Publishing Group, 1995), p. 255.

Success Triangle Point #1—God Is Confident in You

King Solomon of ancient Israel stated the value of putting your confidence in God this way: "For the Lord will be your confidence and will keep your foot from being caught."[6]

It is fascinating to observe how some of the greatest inventors and scientists in history have confidently overcome all kinds of obstacles and enemies with their confidence rooted in God. God declared that all His creation was "good," including humanity. He believed in us, had confidence in our abilities to care for the earth, and formed us in His image and likeness. God believed in us so much that He turned the stewardship and care of the earth over to us!

Success Triangle Point #2— Be Confident in Yourself

6 Proverbs 3:26 (NIV).

Virtually all successful people share this one characteristic—*a confident belief in themselves.* You must be confident in the fact that the God who created you also put within you the abilities and talents necessary for you to succeed. Your personal faith in God must translate into a confidence in yourself. You must believe in your own ability to succeed and accomplish extraordinary things in life. You know deep within yourself that there is a reason why you were created. You do not want to leave this planet without accomplishing something significant in your life. Your personal will to succeed and win in this game called life is what gives you the winner's edge.

CONFIDENCE COACHING SOLUTION

In order to inspire confidence in others you must first have confidence in yourself.

Decide now to have confidence in your abilities, your decision making, your wisdom, your ability to discern right and wrong, your knowledge, and your gut feelings.

Success Triangle Point #3—Be Confident in Others

Confidence. There is perhaps no stronger steel than well-founded self-belief: the knowledge that your preparation is complete, that you have done all things possible to ready your-

self and your organization for the competition, whatever form it comes in.[7]

—John Wooden, basketball coach

Many people complain that no one believes in them. Well, how can someone believe in them if they don't believe in themselves?

Increasing your personal level of confidence empowers you to believe in other people and to inspire confidence in them. Your confidence in God and in yourself will inspire confidence in other people. It's difficult for those who do not have confidence in themselves to have much confidence in others.

Past hurts from others may have caused you to mistrust people. Success coach Wolf J. Rinke writes, "If you mistrust your employees, you'll be right three percent of the time. If you

---

7 John Wooden, *Wooden on Leadership* (New York: McGraw-Hill, 2005), p. 51.

trust people until they give you a reason not to, you'll be right ninety-seven percent of the time." In the words of John C. Maxwell, those are pretty good odds.[8]

Finding people you can believe in and encouraging them will inspire them, and they will reciprocate by putting their confidence in you. Placing confidence in other people is a very important leg on your triangle of success. Why? Because you will accomplish only a fraction of your potential by working alone. If you do everything alone and never partner with other people, you will create barriers to unleashing your full potential. Basketball coach John Wooden said, "The man who puts the ball through the hoop has ten hands." Always remember—*championships are never won by a winning player, only by a winning team.*

CONFIDENCE COACHING SOLUTION
Nobody succeeds alone!

In order to succeed, you will have to put your confidence in other people's intelligence, abilities, and talents. You must reject the myth that one person can achieve something great. Nobody succeeds alone! It takes teamwork to make the dream work. Even the Lone Ranger partnered with Tonto. Be assured, there are no real Terminators or Rambos who can

8 Wolf J. Rinke, *Winning Management: Fail-Safe Strategies for Building High-Performance Organizations* (Clarksville, MD: Achievement Publishers, 1997).

single-handedly take on an entire city or nation. That only happens in Hollywood!

Everyone needs other people to help them achieve their dreams. John Maxwell made a profound statement when he said, "One is too small a number to achieve greatness."[9]

Business leaders lose confidence in people when people do not do what was asked of them. Then many leaders stop delegating and get the mentality that "If I want something done right, I need to do it myself." This mentality paralyzes leaders from fulfilling their full potential.

The bigger your personal dream is, the more you need the input, energy, time, and help of other qualified people. If your dream can be fulfilled by yourself, then your dream is too small. If you want to accomplish something big, link up with other people and create your personal dream team.

> No one can whistle a symphony. It takes an orchestra to play it.
>
> —Halford Luccock, Christian writer

Start developing a true love for people. Those whom you decide to include in your circle of love will help you. The people you exclude from your circle of love can hurt you. You must eliminate all negative attitudes toward other people, such as jealousy, envy, hatred, resentment, and cyni-

9 John C. Maxwell, *The 17 Indisputable Laws of Teamwork: Embrace Them and Empower Your Team* (Nashville: Thomas Nelson and Sons, 2001), p. 2.

cism. These negative attitudes toward others will never bring you success.

If you don't put your confidence in God, you may become arrogant and cocky. If you don't develop confidence in yourself, you will live a defeated lifestyle. If you lose your confidence in other people, you will limit your potential and always be uncertain of other people's motives and their ability to perform.

"Confidence is contagious. So is lack of confidence," said Vince Lombardi, the head coach of the Green Bay Packers who led them to six division titles, five NFL championships, and two Super Bowl games. Confidence begets confidence. If you have confidence in God, confidence in yourself, and confidence in others, you will inspire others to have confidence in each of these areas as well.

Others Will Become Confident in You

People will tolerate honest mistakes, but if you violate their trust, you will find it very difficult to ever regain their confidence. That is one reason that you need to treat trust as your most precious asset. You may fool your boss but you can never fool your colleagues or subordinates.

—Craig Weatherup, PepsiCo chairman and CEO

The willingness of people to put their confidence in you as a leader is an important key for success in your personal life and in business.

Your success and effectiveness as a person lie in your leadership abilities. As you increase your ability to lead others, your influence, success, and income will naturally increase. In order to build something significant, you have to build a team of people around you.

How? They must trust you.

Lose trust and you lose your ability to lead people. People will listen to someone they know, but they will follow someone they trust. "The reason you have to say 'trust me' is that you haven't earned it and are forced to ask for it—bad move."[10]

Build Confidence in Others

How do we build confidence in others? *By developing others.* People won't be there if you don't develop relationships with them before you need their help. What does developing people mean? Developing people means:

1. I value them.
2. I commit time to them.
3. I mentor them.
4. I equip them.
5. I empower them.

10 Jeffrey Gitomer, *Jeffrey Gitomer's Little Teal Book of Trust: How to Earn It, Grow It, and Keep It to Become a Trusted Advisor in Sales, Business, and Life* (Upper Saddle River, NJ: FT Press, 2008), p. i.

Your confidence in others will develop their trust and confidence in you. Give and it will be given back to you in abundance. You will reap what you sow. In giving confidence, you will maximize your confidence. Confidence builds with the *Law of Addition*. The Law of Addition simply states that leaders add value by serving others. Here's what I want you to ask yourself as a leader—of a family, business, social organization, Bible study—no matter your leadership role:

- Since I've been leading, are things better or worse for others?
- Am I adding or subtracting value from them?
- Are the people better off because I'm a leader?
- Am I taking others to a higher level?

Leadership isn't how far we advance *ourselves*, but how far we advance *others*. Retired army general Norman Schwarzkopf said, "When you help others climb a hill, you will get closer to the top yourself." You are either adding or subtracting. If you're adding to others, it's intentional; if you are subtracting from others, I think it's unintentional.

You become trustworthy by giving your confidence away to others. A confident leader is someone who has won the trust and confidence of others.

The more you perform, and the more success you have, and the more wisdom you convey over time, the more confidence others will have in you. Confidence comes only as a result of performance over time. A leader who keeps making good decisions and produces great results builds up his or her confidence bank. However, when a leader continues to make one bad decision after another, the confidence level goes down and people do not want to follow them.

Now let's turn in the next chapter to building trust in others through exemplifying confidence, competence, and character.

America's Confidence Coach Reminds You . . .

- God + (You + Confidence) + Other People = You Can Accomplish Anything.
- Your roots start with a "good" image.
- When you make God your partner in life and vocation, your confidence will take a quantum leap.
- Give the gift of confidence.
- Destroy criticism with success.
- When you make your mark in the world, look out for people with big erasers.
- Confident people refuse to make excuses.
- Nobody succeeds alone!

Give confidence away, and people will give you their confidence. You reap what you sow. Start empowering others and move toward your success. Take these steps now . . .

CONFIDENCE MAKEOVER STEPS NOW!

5-Star Confidence Giver

ENCOURAGEMENT   APPRECIATION   AFFIRMATION   RECOGNITION   REINFORCEMENT

★ Encouragement

What water is to a plant, encouragement is to the soul. Encouragement is a gift that keeps on giving. People need encouragement more than they need your criticism. Encouragement recognizes, accepts, affirms, and lets a person know that they are valuable simply because they exist. Encouragement doesn't manipulate because it isn't about performance, it's about essence. You are valuable, and it's okay for you to be who you were made to be.

Do you give people courage to try new things, to try again, to believe in a future that is bigger and better than their present? Encouragement means giving people confidence in the present and for the future. Being an encourager is about believing in people before they succeed.

I can go a whole year on one encouraging word.

—Mark Twain

Say often and continually to others in whom you are building confidence:

- *You can do it.*
- *You can make it.*
- *You are smart.*
- *You are doing a great job.*

★ Appreciation

Appreciation is simply saying thank you to others.

- *Thank you for being in my life.*
- *Thank you for helping me.*
- *Thank you for doing this with excellence.*
- *Thank you for your support on this project.*
- *Thank you for coming in early and staying late.*

★ Affirmation

Affirmation is acknowledging your appreciation for a person's personal abilities or strengths.

- *You are really creative. You are a great organizer.*
- *You are really gifted with your hands.*
- *You are a great communicator.*
- *You are an amazing leader.*

★ Recognition

Recognition is expressing your awareness of another person's accomplishments.

- *You built a great business.*
- *You wrote a great book.*
- *You did a great job on the annual financial report.*
- *You have built a great team.*

★ Reinforcement

Reinforcement is an act performed to strengthen approved behavior. Most leaders and organizations spend most of their time telling people what they do wrong. How about rewarding people who do what is right and exemplify positive behaviors? You can empower people with confidence by rewarding them with gifts of appreciation. These gifts do not have to be extravagant. One of my clients knows I like M&M peanuts. He buys me some whenever I visit his offices, and it makes me feel good about him. I naturally want to do a great job for him. He gets a great return on an investment of less than $1. Try these reinforcing actions . . .

- *Thank-you cards*
- *Flowers for your wife or to a friend from you and your spouse*
- *Candy*
- *Gift cards for a person's favorite restaurant*
- *Money*

Chapter 8

THE CONFIDENCE TO LEAD

OVER the years, numerous people have asked me how I got started in the speaking, coaching, and writing business. The journey actually started while I was running my organization and approaching total burnout. I was a one-man show doing everything in my organization. In my leadership conferences I called myself "SUPER KEITH." If anything needed doing, it was Super Keith to the rescue. The day my life changed was when I went to another organization and saw the CEO actually allowing others to do the work. I thought to myself, *I can't even get a handful of people to work like that for me.* At the end of the meeting with the CEO, I was given a cassette tape that featured John Maxwell on leadership. After listening to the tape, I realized I had to develop and grow my leadership competence.

Up until that moment, I never saw myself as a leader. I thought, like most people, that leaders are just "naturally born," and I was not fortunate enough to be chosen. However, this challenged me to become a leader because I now realized that leadership is a skill that can be developed.

Leadership is both taught and caught. One of my mentors, John Kelly, is a natural leader; he was raised by a father who built some of the largest bridges in America. As his father modeled leadership skills, John caught those skills that he needed. However, in my childhood, I did not have a role-model father from whom I could catch leadership skills; so I had to be taught.

Most people do not realize how important it is to learn leadership skills. In order to lead, you must be willing to get out front—to be assertive, bold, willing to take risks, and secure in your own skin. Power, influence, and financial rewards go to the person who will take a step out from the timid crowd of followers and have the confidence to point the way into the future. Developing yourself as a confident leader is the solution to reinventing your life, exploding your business, and skyrocketing your income.

In order to lead, you must be willing to climb out on the edge of the branch where all the fruit is. Followers hug the trunk of the tree because they are afraid to step out onto the limb. *Lead* connotes "being out front." It takes confidence, *chutzpah*, to get out front!

Learn About Leadership from Leaders

Caught up in a leadership vacuum, people will follow any-body who is willing to get in front. If those who are trying to lead are poor examples, they can cause some serious damage to those who are following them. History gives us many stories of people who produced both good and bad examples from which we can learn. The truism that fits here is "Those who do not know history are apt to repeat it." You can learn from the failures of history's leaders and even those leaders around you. Take the time to sit down with somebody who has failed dramatically but is now stronger than ever and ask, "How did you get to this point in life?" You can also learn from success. Ask a successful leader, "How did you do it?" Leaders love to talk about themselves and share their experiences and wisdom.

Everyone will be remembered for the example they left behind—good or bad. Make sure you are remembered as a good one.

I can categorize everyone on earth into three "success" categories:

1. **No Success:** These people will go to their graves and never taste the fruit of success. The FUD in their lives keep them from taking the first step in their journey toward success. These people live their entire lives in a continual struggle to survive. They are inward-focused be-

cause all they can think about is themselves and how they are going to pay their bills.

2. **Temporary Success:** These people experience a level of success. Their confidence and competence has moved them up the ladder of success. However, their success is only temporary due to their lack of character. Eventually, their character causes them to slip off the mountain of success to crash and burn back into the valley of survival.

3. **Lasting Success:** These people become and remain successful throughout their entire lifetimes. Yes, they may experience temporary setbacks or even horrific failures, but they have the confidence and character to rebound, to maintain success, and to push beyond mere success to make a lasting impact and leave an impressive legacy for others to follow.

What quality do Jesus Christ, Gandhi, Abraham Lincoln, Winston Churchill, Mother Teresa, Billy Graham, Margaret Thatcher, Zig Ziglar, Ken Blanchard, Coach John Wooden, and George Foreman have in common?

* They are considered by many as world-class leaders.
* The impact of their lives will last for generations.
* They have (or had) high moral character and reputation.
* They have the power of the 3 Cs—extreme levels of *confidence, competence,* and *character* in their professions. They

do (or did) what they love—not for money or fame. They focused their energy in one direction and found that money comes as a by-product.

The Leadership Triangle

Next we will examine the Leadership Triangle, which is another part of the whole Confidence Solution Triangle shown at the beginning of the book:

The World-Class Leadership Triangle

Point 1—Confidence

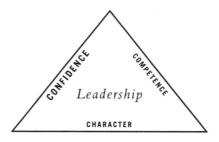

Why is the lion considered the king of the jungle? Because he's the biggest, fastest, prettiest, hardest-working animal in the jungle? No! So why is he the king and on top? Because he's the most confident! What I have discovered is that this truth in the jungle is also true in the financial, business, and cultural jungles in which we live.

I love leadership, and I love history, and one of my favorite people to read about is Harry Truman, who becomes a greater president in the eyes of many the longer he is gone. During his bid for the presidency in 1948, no one gave him a shot to win against challenger Thomas Dewey. During the campaign, Truman asked a man in the crowd how he intended to vote. "Mr. Truman," the man said, "I wouldn't vote for you if yours were the only name on the ballot." Truman turned to an aide and said, "Put him down as doubtful."[1]

Confidence is one of your most valuable assets, and more is always better. Confidence breeds successful leaders. Confident leaders possess more:

- Happiness! More Money!
- Creative Ideas! More Solutions to Problems!
- Success! More Power!
- Relationships! More Fun!

There are nearly seven billion people in the world. Young and old. Rich and poor. They come from different walks of life. They have different nationalities, cultures, and languages. But they all have one need in common—CONFIDENCE. They need the confidence that can empower them to live life to its fullest.

---

1 "Here is what I know about leaders: The great leaders are confident," *Success*, February 2010, p. 18.

*Successful people do habitually what
unsuccessful people do occasionally.*

Everybody wants to have more confidence, more success, more money, and more fun. Right? It is not really "super hard" to obtain these things. If you buy into the myth that gaining more confidence is hard, you will not even try to obtain it. Obtaining more confidence, success, money, and fun is not a matter of working harder, it is a matter of creating the right success habits. What becomes a habit will become easy in time.

The success of your future is hidden in your daily habits. You do not determine your future; you determine your daily habits. Your daily habits ultimately determine your future.

What Is a Habit?

A habit is an unconscious behavior requiring no effort. A habit is something that you do every day that becomes easy. You don't even have to think about it—it's something you do automatically. Let me illustrate. You have developed a daily habit of brushing your teeth. This daily habit has produced a mouth full of healthy, sparkling white teeth. Your daily habit of brushing your teeth produced the future condition of the health of your teeth. Some people have not developed this daily habit. Therefore, they will most likely lose most of their teeth before they die.

The outcome of a bad habit usually does not show up until later in life. You can trace every failure in your life to a bad habit that you permitted to occur daily in your past—in your mind, actions, home, or life. You see, your daily habits determine the quality of your lifestyle for the future.

Every Olympic champion knows the results of good daily habits. Good daily habits not only sharpen a champion's mind and body but they also produce a great side effect—confidence. The Olympic champion knows what his or her body will do when it is called upon to perform. Motivational speakers know that they are communicating effectively when they approach the podium. They have confidence in what they can do because of their daily habits.

CONFIDENCE COACHING SOLUTION

Confident people have confidence-producing habits.

Successful people have successful habits. Confident people have developed confident habits. Successful people do daily what unsuccessful people do occasionally. Developing new habits will take some time. Some people say that it takes a minimum of twenty-one days to create a new habit. For the next twenty-one days, I want you to work on projecting an "I am confident" attitude. The person who has developed good daily habits is confident that good things will happen to him instead of bad.

What Confidence Cannot Do for You

1. Your confidence cannot make up for a lack of competence. Some people confuse competence, which is a function of skill, with confidence, which is a function of attitude and beliefs.
2. Your confidence cannot make up for a lack of experience.

My confidence comes from my age and experience. It is natural as a young person to lack self-confidence, but as we grow older, we realize that we may not care so much about how others view us and that we should be willing to trust our own judgment day-to-day. Experience in performing our jobs clearly increases our confidence level.
—Sandra Day O'Connor, U.S. Supreme Court Justice

CONFIDENCE COACHING SOLUTION
Long-term experience births confidence.

3. Your confidence cannot change the facts. If you are six feet eight inches tall and can't ride a horse beyond a gallop, then being a professional jockey is the wrong career choice for you. Now, if you change your mind and have the talent

and desire to be an NBA guard—that career choice is a real possibility.

If you don't like something, change it. If you can't change it, change your attitude. Don't complain.

—Maya Angelou

4. "Your confidence cannot replace personal development. A time comes when you need to stop waiting for the man you want to become and start being the man you want to be."—Bruce Springsteen
5. Your Confidence Thermostat will not stay on High automatically.

Confidence Solution Axioms

- *Confidence is built by focusing on your successes.*
- *Competence is built by focusing on your strengths.*
- *Character is built by focusing on your weakness.*

Now let's turn to the second point on the triangle for world-class leaders: competence.

Point 2 — Competence

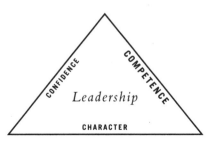

The success of your future is shaped by your passion to increase your competence.

CONFIDENCE COACHING SOLUTION

Your professional career will only rise to the level of your competence. You will rarely be promoted beyond your competence levels.

Lisa Lane Brown played ringette for Team Canada for ten years, winning three world championships. In her book *The Courage to Win*, she says:

> *Competence is having superior technique. There are proven success principles governing money, relationships, and career. When you learn them and then internalize them, you develop superior technique . . . The future belongs to the competent. To win, you need superior technique. Few people train themselves long enough to discover how excellent they can truly be.*[2]

2 Lisa Lane Brown, *The Courage to Win* (Calgary: Lisa Brown Associates, 2008), p. 19.

When your confidence increases, your competence increases at the same time. It is important to understand the relationship and synergy between confidence and competence.

* Competence: The ability to do something.
* Confidence: Your belief about your competence.

Confidence without competence can be a very dangerous combination. An absolute recipe for disaster consists of people who lack competence yet have unjustified confidence. For example, you can be confident that you can fly an airplane. However, if you tried to fly an airplane with no training, your outcome would spell DISASTER!

Conversely, competent people who have tremendous skills, wisdom, and understanding yet lack confidence will never act on what they know. I had the competence to run ten miles with my track coach. However, I did not have the confidence in my abilities to achieve the goal of becoming a winning track-and-field athlete. Competent people without confidence will end up stuck where they are because they refuse to act.

Therefore, you need both competence and confidence to operate and perform at your full potential. Confidence in the end result can fuel the training and equipping that competence requires. Muhammad Ali said it this way: "I hated every minute of training, but I said, 'Don't quit. Suffer now and live the rest of your life as a champion.'" In another arena, Dolly

Parton added this perspective: "I have more confidence than I do talent, and of the two, confidence is the main achiever of success."

CONFIDENCE COACHING SOLUTION

Confidence without competence is dangerous.

For years I had conditioned my mind to think *I can't.* So I would not attempt to do anything new in my life. Once I realized this was negative programming, I reset my mind-set by constantly telling myself, in challenging circumstances or when trying something new, *Yes, I can!*

A few days before going to a conference, my wife mentioned that she needed a haircut before we left. However, the beauty salon was booked for the week, and she could not get an appointment. At that time, a popular hairstyle was to have your hair shaved short in the back. Well, with my new "Yes, I can!" attitude I sold her on the idea that I could take the trimmers and cut her hair for her. As I started with a #4 comb on the trimmer, I had difficulty cutting her hair, so I thought I would try to freehand without the guard. Well, you guessed it. The trimmer slipped and took a section of hair all the way down to her scalp.

I had all the confidence in the world. The problem: I did not have any competence.

One's only security in life comes from doing something uncommonly well.

—Abraham Lincoln

The secret of power is the method by which the fire of youth is translated into the knowledge of experience. Competence is attained through hard work, increasing skill, and the pursuit of excellence.

Every study of high-achieving men and women proves that greatness in life is only possible when you become outstanding at your chosen field. The foundation of lasting self-confidence and self-esteem is excellence, mastery of your work.

—Brian Tracy, business authority

CONFIDENCE COACHING SOLUTION

Invest in your most valuable asset—you!

All the confidence in the world is meaningless if you do not have the knowledge it takes to put your confidence to use. Confidence is built upon what you know. Ignorance breeds fear; the more you learn about your subject, the less power fear has over you. When you increase information, you increase confidence. Learn all there is to know about your field of business: daily operations, customers, competitors, services, and product lines. Invest in yourself, your education, and the tools you need to acquire knowledge. Also invest in relationships; surround yourself with people who have wisdom, knowledge, and understanding.

How will knowing more about all these things help you gain more self-confidence? That is very simple. If you knew every imaginable answer about your business, you would never be afraid of any conceivable question that a supervisor, client, customer, or fellow employee might ask. You would be an expert in the eyes of your clients, work associates, and your boss. Most important, you would be an expert in your own eyes. Would this make you more self-confident? Absolutely!

Make it your personal goal to become an authority at what you do. When people come to you for answers, you know that you have become an expert in your field.

Becoming an Expert Formula:
$$R + S + 5Y = 5\%$$

Becoming an expert is easy. Yes, I said *easy*—if you have the right formula. I learned a simple formula to skyrocket my income by becoming an expert, and it has helped me to become known as America's #1 Confidence Coach.

Here are the details of the formula: Read (R) one hour a day about your subject (S) or your field of work for five years (Y) and you will rise to the top 5 percent in your field.

Do you want to increase your income? If so, remember, the market will pay an expert wage for an expert. If you don't like your income, you can do something about it by becoming an expert.

CONFIDENCE COACHING SOLUTION

Be a lifelong student. The more you learn, the more you earn, and the more self-confidence you will have.

Make a decision today that you are going to prepare yourself to become an expert at what you do. You are going to know more about your field of business than any other person knows about your business. This is a big decision. It will take a great amount of personal pursuit, study, and effort. Here are five easy keys to help you prepare for expert status.

KEY 1. READ AN HOUR EVERY DAY ABOUT YOUR CHOSEN FIELD.

Charlie "Tremendous" Jones, author of *Life Is Tremendous*, says, "You will be the same person in five years except for the people you meet and the books you read."[3] If you take the time to read one book every month about your industry or desired profession, in ten years you will have read 120 books. That puts you in the top 1 percent of your field and guarantees your success. The person who does not read is no better off than the person who can't. The person who has knowledge and does not apply it is no better off than the person who

3 Charlie Jones, *Life Is Tremendous* (Carol Stream, IL: Tyndale House Publishers, 1968).

is ignorant. Remember this, all the books you have not read will not help you a bit! Become committed to becoming a lifetime learner. When you're green, you grow, when you're ripe, you rot.

KEY 2. TURN YOUR CAR INTO A UNIVERSITY ON WHEELS.

Listen to educational audio programs in your car. The average person drives between 12,000 and 25,000 miles per year, which works out to spending between 500 and 1,000 hours per year in the car. You can become an expert in your field by simply listening to educational audio programs as you drive from place to place. Many stores sell audiotapes, CDs, and videotapes featuring top personal-development trainers and business leaders.

KEY 3. ATTEND SEMINARS GIVEN BY EXPERTS IN YOUR FIELD.

Learn from the experts. Ask them questions, write them letters, read their books, read their articles, and listen to people with proven track records in the area in which you want to be successful.

KEY 4. TAKE ADDITIONAL COURSES AND LEARN EVERYTHING YOU POSSIBLY CAN.

Pursue an advanced degree or take some intensive training classes. You can become an expert and gain additional self-confidence if you are willing to pay the price of extra effort.

KEY 5. SEARCH THE INTERNET.

We are living in the information age. The Internet is a wonderful source for finding information. Add your name to some mailing lists of organizations or groups of people in your professional field. A huge amount of terrific information is out there waiting for you.

Point 3—Character

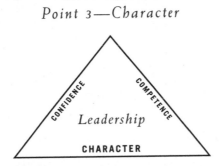

Your competence or talents are sometimes a gift, but your character is a choice. Character is the collection of inner qualities, principles, and beliefs that determine your response regardless of circumstances.

CONFIDENCE COACHING SOLUTION

Confidence and competence will take you to the top,
but it is your character that will keep you there.

What quality were these people lacking? Richard Nixon, Hitler, Jimmy Swaggart, Britney Spears, Tiger Woods, Michael Vick, Mike Tyson, Bill Clinton, Enron executives—

they all lacked *character*! They were all at the top of their game, but then because of their lack of character they lost respect, the privilege of being good examples, and the ability to be effective leaders. Good, strong character supports your competence levels.

Character is essential to the Confidence Solution. Being a person of character gives people someone to attach themselves to and rely upon. A man took his young daughter to a carnival, and she immediately ran over to a booth and asked for cotton candy. As the attendant handed her a huge ball of it, the father asked, "Sweetheart, are you sure you can eat all that?" "Don't worry, Dad," she answered. "I'm a lot bigger on the inside than on the outside." That's what real character is—being bigger on the inside.[4]

Character has incredible value. True wealth and success comes from character. Succeeding in business or life at the expense of your character will leave you no more fulfilled than living in poverty. Competence without character is like a school bus slowly heading for the ditch, and when the bus crashes, many people end up getting hurt. World-class leaders—whether in the home, business, community, church, or internationally—prioritize the development of their inward character above the outward trappings of success, power, and money.

Reputation is like a shadow; sometimes it follows you and

4 John C. Maxwell, *The 21 Indispensable Qualities of a Leader: Becoming the Person Others Will Want to Follow* (Nashville: Thomas Nelson Business, 1999), p. 7.

sometimes it goes ahead of you, but it never leaves you. When I am teaching on character in my leadership conferences, I ask, "When I say the name Bill Clinton, what first comes to your mind?" Almost everybody in the audience responds in unison "Monica Lewinski!" Nobody mentions the economy we had under his leadership. Nobody mentions the fact that he was a great networker with one of the largest Rolodexes of any president.

Your reputation is who people think you are, but your character is who you know you really are. If you focus on building strong character, you will not have to worry about your reputation—it will automatically take care of itself. Warren Buffet said, "It takes twenty years to build a reputation and five minutes to ruin it. If you think about that, you'll do things differently."[5]

Every failure in life can be traced back to a compromise of character. I have learned this lesson myself. Almost every failure or mistake I have made in the past can be traced back to a time when I compromised my character. I am thankful my past issues were not displayed on CNN or Fox News. Your character is your moral compass set on doing what's right and being your best. Character, not charisma, is what the foundation of your success is built on. When your wonderful charm wears off, all you have left is character. In refusing to be changed by either the world around them, other

5 Robb Thompson, *Total Life Makeover* (Tinley Park, IL: RTI, 2009), p. 5.

people, or circumstances, people of character do what's right, knowing it will change the world.

I have been fortunate to stay in some of the nicest hotel chains in the world such as the W, the Ritz Carlton, the Four Seasons, and many others. In the hotel industry, these hotels have a rating based on their level of excellence. The highest rating is five-star. Would you rate your character five-star? Examine yourself with each of the following qualities.

Star 1—Decision

Character starts with a decision to lift your personal moral standards. In order for a hotel to get five-star status, management decides before the foundation of the building is even poured that they are going to have a higher standard than other hotels.

Character is the values and principles instilled within your life that govern every decision. It is the mental and moral attributes that define you. Confident people do not put their character on sale.

Star 2—Truth

Truth must be embraced in order to have great character. It is faddish today to tell lies. Politicians get caught in lies. We tell jokes about lawyers who cannot tell the truth. Survivors on reality television shows are rewarded by cheating, conniving, and lying their way to a victory—and millions of people watch every week. Lying has become a pop culture art form.

But honesty is important in every aspect of life, because when truth is absent, morality has nothing to stand on. People and nations are not great because of their wealth but because of their commitment to truth. Nigeria is known worldwide for its corruption. Telling the truth can sometimes be the hardest thing you can do, but it can also be one of the most liberating things you can do.

You cannot build a foundation of success and prosperity on a lie. Your lie may get you what you want in the present, but it will go into the future and cause you to pay a price you did not want to pay. What is wrong and inconsistent with good character cannot be made right, no matter what.

Be careful; we live in a generation in which it is acceptable to lie. Tell the truth anyway.

Truth is always right. Lying is always wrong. When you do what is wrong, it erodes your confidence.

Fill your heart with truth. There is nothing trustworthy, consistent, or good about a person who always lies. Truth must be sought out, studied, learned, and rehearsed. Tell yourself the truth. The greatest deception is self-deception. When you lie to yourself, you end up lying to others. The more truthful you become with yourself, the more truthful you become in communicating with others. *Tell the truth and be honest with others.*

A simple definition of honesty is *behavior in words and actions that aims to convey the truth.* Conversely, dishonesty is *a way of speaking or acting that causes people to be misled or deluded.* Always consider the interest of others and not just your own. I say it like this: I would rather you hate me for telling you the truth than for you to like me for telling you a lie. You have heard the truth. Always tell the truth and then you do not have to be worried about what you say; you can communicate with confidence.

Truth is a matter of black and white, not gray. A situation or decision is either right or wrong, good or bad, in or out. The big question: How do you know what is right or wrong? Is it really that hard to figure out? No, not really.

How do you know whether something is the right or wrong thing to do? If you have to ask, it's the wrong thing. You always know the right thing, you only have to ask the question when it is the wrong thing. So do the right thing even when it is unpopular or might cost you money or embarrass you. In the long run, consistently doing the right thing will pay off every time, without exception. Do the right thing with your kids, your spouse, your family, your boss, your employees, your customers, and the stranger in the car next to you or the one you pass on the street. Do the right thing with your taxes too! Never compromise your future success by short-changing your present by doing less than the right thing in every circumstance.

Star 3—Talk

The first week we moved into our new house, I needed to quickly find someone to mow the grass and do much-needed landscaping. I was shocked when I learned that the companies in my area have one-year service contracts. Sign a one-year service contract just to mow my grass every week? Life had certainly changed since the day I was a young boy cutting grass in the summer for $5 a yard.

Once upon a time there was a day when a person's word coupled with a handshake was a firm bond. Welcome to the new era of contracts, service agreements, and lawsuits. Why? Because people do not have the character to do what they say or promise.

The days have changed. Today we have to have everything in writing. Be a person of your word if you sign a contract. Do what you say you are going to do and do more. The motto I work hard to live by is "Under-promise and over-perform."

Keep your promises and your word. Leaders are defined by the quality of their actions, not the rambling of their words; therefore make it the rule to always under-promise and over-perform.

Your words are continually educating others around you. Let them create a portrait of character, enthusiasm, and confidence. Character is truthfulness. It is doing what you say you will do.

Star 4—Walk

Old saying: "Don't talk the talk, but walk the walk." I learned a long time ago not to watch people's mouths (what they say) but to watch their feet. I like the old saying "If it walks like a duck and quacks like a duck . . . it's a duck."

Character is a habit the confident person exercises every day by always doing the right thing even to his or her own detriment. Do what is right, and you will feel right. Character will cause you to fight for what is right.

What you do speaks so loud that I cannot hear what you say.
—Ralph Waldo Emerson

Pride will break your stride. After several months of silence after he was caught cheating on his wife, Tiger Woods said in his first statement to the public that he "felt like he could do whatever he wanted." Pride of achievement or success can cause you to feel like you are invincible. You can feel like you are so "important" that you are above the law. And when you think you are above the law, you will break the law. So ask yourself these questions:

- What do I do in moments of intense pressure to compromise?
- Do I do the easy thing or the right thing?
- What if a convenient lie could cover a mistake?
- Would I tell a little white lie?
- How far would I go to win a client?

Star 5—Stand

If you do not know what you stand for, you will fall for anything. Insecure people who have no inner character eventually become slaves to their outward circumstances. They have weak internal confidence and character; therefore, they do not have the guts to stand up for what they think is right. They will give in to the temptations and pressures that those who lack character offer. Their character is built on "situational ethics," which are based on the thought *If it feels right . . . do it.*

Character isn't how we act when life is going the way we want it. It is revealed when your life is far from what you really want. Character is developed when you decide to stand strong against unethical behavior. In fact, all of humanity is bent toward unethical behavior. That is why we must not allow ourselves to lower our standards.

Don't let up. Don't allow yourself to cut corners or achieve any standard of living in an unethical manner. Be true to yourself, and you will quickly attract true success to your life. Character is an internal quality that is fed by external sources; the books you read, the music you listen to, the people you hang around with help build or destroy your character. Evil companionships corrupt good character. Harvard University's Dr. David McClelland diligently researched the qualities and characteristics of high achievers in our society. What he discovered was an individual's choice of "reference group" (the people with whom he or she habitually associates) was far more important than any other single factor when determining success or failure.[6]

Character is comprised of the values and principles instilled within your life that govern every decision. It is the mental and moral attributes that define you. Good character refers to the virtue, the self-discipline, and the honorable constitution an individual possesses. It also denotes moral strength. Although these principles do not always dictate a single "moral" course of action, they do provide a standard for evaluation when deciding between conflicting options.

6 Ibid., p. 81.

The law of character says that the outcome of your life is completely dependent upon the strength of your moral fiber. It is the foundation of all life. No contractor would begin to build without the foundation passing inspection. The longevity of any building depends on the strength of its foundation. Do you see the correlation between building a skyscraper and building a life? Do you see the vital role character plays in your career success?

Don't Stand Alone

Relationships are built on character. You cannot sustain a relationship unless both parties are committed to character. I like to say it like this: Integrity is the foundation upon which your life's work is built. Always prize principle above relationship; otherwise, you soon compromise when others around you pressure you to do so.

I can fail all by myself. I need a strong moral team of people around me that will keep me right. Does your team encourage you to be better?

It is important that you surround yourself with people who are just as committed to being five-star people as you are. The old saying says it well: "Bad company corrupts good moral character."[7] Your good character most often won't

7 1 Corinthians 15:33b (NIV).

change the bad character of another, but bad character will most often stain your commitment to five-star character. Be serious about your commitment to living a five-star lifestyle, and surround your life with those who are serious as well. If you make a commitment to embrace the five-star character, will it automatically make you rich and successful? Of course not.

CONFIDENCE COACHING SOLUTION

Character will keep you on top as long as you have the confidence and competence to get there.

I have had a mentor for twenty years who exemplifies incredible character in his personal life and in our relationship. He has been married to the same woman for more than forty years and is a great father to his children. Whenever we are together, he starts talking about the subject of character, which I appreciate because sometimes I can be a real "character." This man reads about character and gives lectures about character often. I have learned that you can have character, but if you do not have confidence and competence as well, you are not going to go anywhere.

Unfortunately, my mentor lacks competence. He still speaks like they did in the 1950s. He has not transitioned himself from a speaker to a great communicator. Also, his confidence level is very low. When I start talking to him about leadership and creating a strategic plan for his organization for the future, his insecurities surface and he tells me "I just don't know how to see or plan for the future." This man has all kinds of character, but he lacks confidence and competence to become a world-class leader.

John Maxwell proposes some excellent questions for self-examination when considering character. Ask yourself:

Am I going to make an emotional decision? Pressure creates tension, and tension can make for some emotional moments. Some people have a hard time in such situations, and they make poor decisions that impact themselves or others. How can I guard against that?

Am I going to compromise the truth? Some people find it impossible to admit making a mistake. Am I willing to stick with the truth even when I don't like it?

Am I going to take shortcuts? Someone once said that the longest distance between two points is a shortcut. While that may be true, pressure tempts us to consider shortcuts when we otherwise wouldn't. Am I willing to fight to do what's right?

Am I going to keep my commitments? Molière said, "Men are alike in their promises. It is only in their deeds that they differ." Am I going to keep my word and follow through, even when it hurts?

Am I going to bow to others' opinions? Some people are especially susceptible to the opinions of others. That was true of me the first five years of my career. Will I do what I know is right, even when it is unpopular?

Am I going to make promises I can't keep? Samuel Johnson said, "We ought not to raise expectations which it is not in our power to satisfy. It is more pleasing to see smoke brightening into a flame, than flame sinking into smoke." How am I going to keep my promises from going up in smoke?[8]

The Confidence Solution for leadership combines character, competence, and confidence so you can stay out front as you reinvent yourself, explode your business, and skyrocket your income. Now it's time to turn to the power of attraction as part of your Confidence Solution.

America's Confidence Coach Reminds You . . .

- Successful people do habitually what unsuccessful people do occasionally.
- Champions are people in whom confidence has become visible.
- Set your personal goal: I want to increase my confidence!
- Confident people have confidence-producing habits.
- Long-term experience births confidence.
- Confidence without competence is dangerous.

8 John C. Maxwell, *Ethics 101: What Every Leader Needs to Know* (New York: Center Street, 2003), pp. 58–59.

- Invest in your most valuable asset—you!
- Be a lifelong student. The more you learn, the more you earn, and the more self-confidence you will have.
- Confidence and competence will take you to the top, but it is your character that will keep you there.
- Character starts with a confident decision.
- Character will keep you on top as long as you have the confidence and competence to get there.

CONFIDENCE MAKEOVER STEPS NOW!

Answer these questions and take action to implement them.

1. What areas of your character need to be straightened out?
2. Have you been honest in your business and personal dealings?
3. Write down five steps you can take to increase your competency level in an area in which you know you are lacking. Take those steps within the next month.

_____

_____

_____

_____

_____

_____

_____

Chapter 9

THE CONFIDENCE
TO ATTRACT ATTENTION

∽

MY speaking schedule requires me to spend more than 247 days per year on the road. When some people discover that about me, they sympathetically ask, "Do you have any hobbies?" And my first response is always, "Yes, I love to drive my canary yellow Corvette convertible down along Clearwater Beach. The first thing I do when I get home from a trip is jump into my 'Vette and take a ride."

I will never forget the day I came home from a trip to Spain. Tired and hungry for some Asian food, I escorted my wife to the car and went to our favorite Japanese steakhouse. It felt so good driving down the road with the top down and my hair blowing in the wind. Several times as I made the trip to the steakhouse and stopped at traffic lights, people rolled down their car windows and told me what a nice car I had. Of course, by the time I arrived at my destination, I was feeling on top of the world.

One time I pulled into the restaurant parking lot and noticed a brand-new, deep blue $400,000 Rolls-Royce parked in front. I parked right beside this beautiful piece of machinery. When I went into the restaurant, I was seated next to the owner of the car. I knew something was different about this person because everybody at the restaurant was treating him as if he were a movie star. So I introduced myself, and we shared a handshake. At this point I still did not know who he was, but we had a great time talking.

Who was this mysterious person? Roberto Velázquez Alomar, a former major league baseball player, considered by many to be one of the best second basemen in history. During his career, he won more Gold Gloves than any second baseman in history and also won the second-most Silver Slugger awards for a second baseman.

On our way out of the restaurant, we shared phone numbers and talked about his new Rolls-Royce. By this time, the entire restaurant staff was outside admiring the car. Although my canary yellow Corvette convertible was parked right next to the Rolls-Royce, people were so enraptured with the Rolls-Royce that they didn't even pay attention to my car.

When I got back into my car, I must admit that my pride was a little punctured because no one noticed my bright yellow 'Vette. But as I drove away, a thought came to me: *Both are really nice cars. However, the one with the most value attracts the most attention.*

Attraction comes from increasing your value. Don't go through life invisible! Increase your value; magnify your visibility. Value captures people's attention. If you allow yourself to become invisible, you will eventually become extinct.

Your parents taught you to "stay in" when a rainstorm came. But hiding for shelter is the absolute worst thing you can do when a "lifestorm" comes. We all have a tendency, when hard times come, to hide in our caves waiting for the storm to pass. This is the worst thing you can do! You need to be seen. You need exposure. You need to position yourself for opportunities.

In the midst of one of his dark periods, when the news was filled with stories of his financial demise, Donald Trump talks about the feeling of wanting to hide at home instead of putting on his tuxedo and going to an important gala. He went because he knew he could not possibly gain anything by staying home.[1]

---

1 Dan Kennedy, *No B.S. Wealth Attraction in the New Economy* (Irvine, CA: Entrepreneur Press, 2010), p. 76.

When you are seen and are attractive, things start naturally coming to you. Nobody wakes up attractive! Therefore, attraction must be intentional. If you want opportunities, relationships, and riches to come to you, the Attraction Triangle is a tool you can use to get you there.

The success of your future rests on your ability to influence people to become your friends as quickly as possible. Your network determines your net worth. Your ability to build a successful business is based on your ability to attract high-quality people to your team who know more than you do about their field of expertise.

Do you make a WOW first impression? When you see a Rolls-Royce or a Lamborghini, your internal response is "WOW." In this fast-paced new world, it is more important than ever that you make a fantastic first impression. People have taught in the past that the first thirty seconds determine what kind of impression you make on the person you are meeting. I disagree. I think it is quicker.

The 7/11 Principle

One of my favorite places to stop when I am cruising in my Corvette is the 7-Eleven convenience store because the name reminds me of this life principle:

You have only 7 seconds to make a great first impression.

In 7 seconds people are subconsciously making 11 impressions about you.

They are subconsciously asking in those 7 seconds these 11 things: *Are you . . .*

1. Confident
2. Competent
3. Honest
4. Credible
5. Courteous
6. Attractive
7. Professional
8. Intelligent
9. Friendly
10. Responsible
11. Clean

What happens during the time you first meet someone determines three important things about the relationship and connection in the future:

- **Attraction:** if they like you
- **Antipathy:** if they don't like you
- **Apathy:** if they are indifferent toward you

You will either create a positive impression that will cause the person to be drawn to you and this will open the door of a new relationship, or you will create an impression that will slam the door shut on any future opportunities, leaving you with a negative consequence.

If a person's first impression of you is *antipathy* or *apathy,* you will lose the magnetic *attraction* to establish a relationship and the person will naturally avoid you. You will then have to work twice as hard to change the impression the person has of you so you can gain their confidence—thus defeating the purpose of attraction.

You are always making an impression; the question is *What kind of impression are you making?* Your impression tachometer does not wait for you to get ready. It starts the moment you are seen in a room. Your *seven seconds* start the first time someone meets you, interacts with you, or hears you talking on the phone. You are always communicating to others at three different levels:

- **Visual**—55 percent—dress, physiology, and behavior
- **Vocal**—38 percent—voice levels and tones
- **Verbal**—10 percent—intelligence, grammar, and language

What kind of impression are you making?

Remember, the image a first impression makes is everything for an initial connection with someone else! You are a walking billboard sending off messages about you everywhere you go. You must be intentional about making great impressions every day. Don't wait for others to form their impression of you; decide what kind of impression you want to make. Ask yourself this question: *How do I want people to perceive me?* What word would you use to describe how you want others to view you?

Attraction is an important element in the Confidence Solution to skyrocketing your income. So let's explore the aspects of this important component in your success by using the Attraction Triangle and the Inner You Triangle.

The Attraction Triangle

Point 1—The Inner You

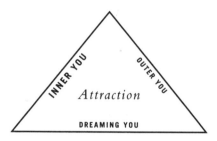

People are hurting. Our world is full of people who have been verbally, sexually, mentally, and physically abused. Millions of people are oppressed by addictions to pornography, drugs, alcohol, cigarettes, overeating, and other things. These people work beside us every day. They walk in hurting, tormented, and bound, and leave hurting, tormented, and bound. Many of these hurting people, deep down inside, want to rebuild their confidence, but they don't know how. So they hide their pains and addictions behind masks and pretend everything is okay. I have always said that the greatest enemy to lasting change is pretending everything is okay when it's not.

Have you ever met a really attractive person and thought *I would like to develop a relationship with that person.* But when you actually got to know the person, you thought *This person is beautiful on the outside, but ugly on the inside.* Looking great on the outside starts by dressing up your inside.

Here are two questions that I ask myself to improve the inner me:

1. What three things make me ugly inside?

My answers:
- Hate
- Ignorance
- Negative attitude

2. What three things make me attractive inside?

My answers:
- Love
- Knowledge
- Positive attitude

There are three aspects to the Inner You so let's use another triangle to look at what makes up the Inner You. We'll get back to the Attraction Triangle and the Outer You and Dreaming You after we discuss how to create the best Inner You possible.

The Inner You Triangle

Point 1—Love

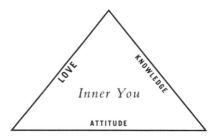

I like the example that Dale Carnegie uses in his classic book, *How to Win Friends and Influence People*:

> *Why read this book to find out how to win friends? Why not study the technique of the greatest winner of friends the world has ever known? Who is he? You may meet him tomorrow coming down the street. When you get within ten feet of him, he will begin to wag his tail. If you stop and pat him, he will almost jump out of his skin to show you how much he likes you. And you know that behind this show of affection on his part, there are no ulterior motives: He doesn't want to sell you any real estate, and he doesn't want to marry you.*
>
> *Did you ever stop to think that a dog is the only animal*

that doesn't have to work for a living? A hen has to lay eggs, a cow has to give milk, and a canary has to sing. But a dog makes his living by giving you nothing but love.[2]

This is treating others better than yourself. It's the Golden Rule: *Do unto others as you would have them do unto you.* Rabbi Jesus said it this way, paraphrased, "Here is a simple rule-of-thumb guide for behavior: Ask yourself what you want people to do for you, then grab the initiative and do it for them. Add up God's Law and the Prophets and this is what you get."[3]

I love how John Hope Bryant, the founder and CEO of Operation Hope, the first nonprofit, social-investment banking operation in the United States, explains this principle in his book *Love Leadership:*

There are two things in this world: love and fear. What you don't love, you fear. In my teens, I was running my early businesses out of fear. What you don't love, you fear. As we've seen, fear is me-focused.

It is short-term. It is based in greed.

The alternative is love-based prosperity. The third law of love leadership—love makes money—breaks down into a set of interlocking and related goals: creating long-term relationships built on caring for others and in service of a larger good.

2 Dale Carnegie, *How to Win Friends and Influence People* (New York: Pocket Books, 1990), p. 53.

3 Matthew 7:12.

Each goal is guided by love. When you operate this way, the by-product can't help but be prosperity for everyone, which naturally leads to money for you, too.

That's because love always leads to money. Money is nothing more than one of the many by-products of love leadership. That's right: Money, over the long term, is simply another confirmation that you're doing good work. It's a by-product. It's never the product.[4]

If you lead with love for the long term, people will follow you forever, wherever—for their own good as well as yours—and you will be remembered as a person of greatness.

The love of our neighbor is the only door out of the dungeon of self.

—George MacDonald

The key to your Confidence Solution is loving people. Loving people is one of the foundational building blocks to attracting people and building a strong team. Unconditional love means that you continue to love people regardless of their performance. What they do or don't do. It means treating your boss, staff, associates, and clients the way you treat your own family.

---

4 John Hope Bryant, "Love Relationship," *Success Book Summary* (San Francisco: Jossey-Bass, 2009), p. 3.

Do I Really Love People?

Art DeMoss made famous this advice: "Love people and use things—don't love things and use people." Genuine love for others is a critical component of attractiveness. If you love people, they will look past your flaws. But if they sense you don't love them, your imperfections will be an irritant to them.[5]

> *Love is the desire to benefit others even at the expense of self, because love desires to give. Lust desires to benefit self even at the expense of others because lust desires to get.*[6]

CONFIDENCE COACHING SOLUTION
Change your thinking from "Me" to "We."
Just flip the "M."

Selflessness versus Selfishness. Are you thinking of yourself or others? Selflessness is when you lovingly put others first and selfishness is when you are always thinking about yourself and wanting things your way. I remember the first time I had the opportunity to speak before thousands of people. I was feeling nervous. I started thinking about how I looked: *Is my hair combed? Am I dressed right? Is my tie okay? Do I have my*

---

5 Bobb Biehl, "Attractiveness," Bobb Biehl, Executive Mentor, www.bobbbiehl .com.

6 Edwin Louis Cole, *Treasure: Uncover Patterns and Principles That Create Prosperity* (Southlake, TX: Watercolor Books, 2001), p. 41.

zipper zipped? When everything checked out okay, I asked myself, *Did I choose the right color for my PowerPoint presentation? What is the first thing I'm going to say? Will they like my message?*

By the time I was finished going through this internal dialogue, I could tell my confidence was leaving me. Then I remembered what one of my mentors, Bobb Biehl, taught me. I should always focus on the audience and what I can do to help them. Wow, I didn't even realize I was being selfish. I was concerned about me and not my audience. When I started thinking about the needs of the people in the audience, my nervousness left me.

Point 2—Knowledge

My definition for personal development is "Believe in your own worth and future potential enough that you give yourself permission to invest time, effort, and money in preparing yourself for your future."

Have you ever heard the saying "You have to be in the right place at the right time?" Do you believe it? I believe this is a partial truth. I have found that you have to *be* the right person in the right place at the right time.

When you fail to plan, you are planning to fail. When you fail to have a daily plan for personal development, you are planning not to grow. Many people really think they are growing and adding value to themselves by increasing their knowledge, but most are not. When I speak on personal growth in my seminars, I ask people, "How many of you have a detailed reading plan on how you are going to grow mentally in the next year?" I have yet to find a crowd where more than 1 percent raised their hands.

Here is what I have done over the past five years to grow myself as a leadership and confidence expert.

My plan for becoming America's #1 Confidence Coach:

	MORNING	EVENING
Monday	Meditation/devotion/exercise	Read confidence book
Tuesday	Meditation/devotion/exercise	Read confidence book
Wednesday	Meditation/devotion/exercise	Read coaching book
Thursday	Meditation/devotion/exercise	Read consulting book
Friday	Meditation/devotion/exercise	Read leadership book
Saturday	Listen to a CD by one of my mentors	
Sunday	Free Day	

I will be continuing this plan indefinitely. We are *learners for life*. Education is a process. The word *education* comes from the Latin word *educere*, which means to draw out. It is the process of drawing out of us what we did not know was there. Your level of achievement or personal income rarely exceeds your passion for personal development. Some well-known people have said:

I will study, I will prepare, for my time will come.

—Abraham Lincoln

I was studying and learning Africaans . . . for I knew when I was released from prison I would be used to transform this country.

—Nelson Mandela

I do not believe in luck, I believe that success comes when preparation and opportunity meet together.

—Oprah Winfrey

Circumstances may cause interruptions and delays, but never lose sight of your goal. Prepare yourself in every way you can by increasing your knowledge and adding to your experience, so that you can make the most of opportunity when it occurs.

—Mario Andretti, race car driver

Are you adaptable to new knowledge and learning? In today's fast-paced, changing business environment, we must adapt to change to overcome obstacles. Don't get stuck with yesterday's ideas, tools, or technology. Read books, trade magazines, and attend trade shows and seminars to learn new trends in your industry. Plan to adapt ideas quickly that will enhance customer service, product quality, and business efficiency so your income will skyrocket.

You may not be able to do everything now, but start somewhere—now. Adapt now for future business success.

Invest in Yourself

Spend time, effort, and dollars developing your mind and your inner person. If a $20 meal makes your stomach feel good for four hours, think what it could do to your mentality and power-life to invest the $20 in CDs or books that soak your mind.

Buy records and CDs that fill your home and your car with the wisdom of God. Hunters invest in guns. Free spirits invest in motorcycles. Nations buy tanks and weapons. Bodybuilders buy protein shakes. Leaders invest in things that will boost them further toward their goals. The successful person is one who invests in equipping himself. Shipping tycoon Aristotle Onassis said, "The secret of success is to know something nobody else knows."

Most people today are in love with the *image* of success, but they are far less interested in the *process* of becoming successful.

CONFIDENCE COACHING SOLUTION

Nourish your potential by becoming an expert.

Whatever you are, be a good one.

—Abraham Lincoln

Sixty-eight percent of people who consider themselves successful say that in at least one area of their job they are an expert.[7] What is an expert? An expert is defined in *Webster's* as one who has special knowledge of a subject or special skill in a field of action.

It is very important for you to choose just one subject and learn everything you can about it. Many people try to become an expert on many different topics. They live their lives with the philosophy of "don't put all your eggs in one basket" or "you need to learn a little bit about everything so you will have something to fall back on." Both of these statements are motivated by fear. Make a focused effort to become an expert on one topic.

Seven benefits will emerge when you become an expert on one subject:

1. Your confidence will multiply because of increased information.
2. Your confidence toward your dreams and goals will increase.
3. People will listen to your thoughts and perspective because they have less knowledge than you.
4. People will put more confidence in you and your abilities.
5. You will be respected and followed.
6. You will become an invaluable asset to your company.
7. Your knowledge of other subjects will instantly increase.

7 David Niven, Ph.D., *100 Simple Secrets of Happy People: What Scientists Have Learned and How You Can Use It* (New York: HarperOne, 2006), p. 123.

Be a lifelong student. The more you learn, the more you earn, and the more self-confidence you will have.

Make a decision today that you are going to prepare yourself to become an expert at what you do. You are going to know more about your field of business than any other person knows about your business. This is a big decision. It will take a great amount of personal pursuit, study, and effort. It is worth it!

What I do is prepare myself until I know I can do what I have to do.

—Joe Namath, the only quarterback in the NFL to pass for four thousand yards in a fourteen-game season

CONFIDENCE COACHING SOLUTION

Preparation today gives confidence tomorrow.

Your dream will require a high level of confidence. The best way to meet the future is to prepare for it as much as you can.

The secret of success in life is for a man to be ready for his time when it comes.

—Benjamin Disraeli, England's first and only Jewish prime minister

221

Humility Is a Key to Learning

So, if you continue to learn and become an expert, will success make you arrogant and drive people away from you? Humility is not denying how great you are, talking bad about yourself, depreciating your talents, ignoring your achievements, or denying your competence levels. Humility is not thinking less *of* yourself. It is thinking less *about* yourself so you can empower others.

Pride is self-focused. Prideful people think they *know* it all; that is why they do not *have* it all. Humble people want to *learn* it all; that is why they have it all.

Jerry Seinfeld says pride is why so many bookstores have trouble attracting customers: "A bookstore is a 'smarter than you' store. And that's why people are intimidated—because to walk into a bookstore, you have to admit there's something you don't know."[8]

Humility is recognizing you "don't know what you don't know" and deciding to learn. Ed Cole wrote in *Treasure,* "Passion is the folly of youth, pride is the folly of middle age, and prejudice is the folly of old age."[9] Dave Martin in a Facebook post remarked, "What increases your income? The average person reads one book a year; a CEO will average over thirty

8 Jerry Seinfeld, *Sein Language* (New York: Bantam Books, 1993), p. 3.
9 Cole, *Treasure,* p. 46.

books a year. The CEO makes 389 percent more than the average person. What do you think you should start doing immediately?"

When we are proud, we are less likely to seek out experts, mentors, education, and advice. Without fresh ideas on how to win, we fall back into helplessness, convinced that winning is not possible. This is the inspiration for the axiom: "If you keep doing what you've always done, you'll keep getting what you've always gotten."[10]

Keep learning. Invest in yourself. Decide that becoming an expert not only improves you, but is essential in helping others.

Point 3—Attitude

Heather Whitestone McCallum's name has become synonymous with incredible determination and unprecedented achievement. Profoundly deaf since eighteen months of age, she strove to live a normal life, refusing to listen to the voices of discouragement that often confronted her. She ignored the doctor who said she wouldn't develop beyond third-grade abilities, and those who said she would never dance ballet or speak.

On September 17, 1994, Heather became the first woman

10 Lisa Lane Brown, *The Courage to Win* (Calgary: Lisa Brown Associates, 2008), p. 18.

with a disability to be crowned Miss America in the pageant's seventy-five-year history. In that moment, she proved to the world that no obstacle is too big and that with hard work, determination, and God's help, we can accomplish whatever we set out to do. Heather has always believed that the biggest handicap is negative thinking and that people handicap themselves by concentrating only on the negative instead of the positive.

CONFIDENCE COACHING SOLUTION
Get rid of your real handicap—a bad attitude!

The attitude you have about life, people, work, marriage, money, events, and the world around you determines your level of success and happiness. A negative attitude concerning these issues can paralyze you in your tracks. However, a positive attitude can cause you to take massive positive action on any given day. When a person has a right mental attitude, they believe that they can move mountains and achieve the impossible. However, when a person has a wrong mental attitude, even the smallest pebble can stop them from moving forward to achieve success in life.

A study of the Olympics reveals that the difference between the gold or silver medal can be only one-tenth of one second *or less*! Sports psychologists have determined that the difference between one-tenth of a second in success or failure is not athletic ability—but attitude. Chris Evert was one of the greatest tennis players of her time and she said, "The thing that separates good players from great ones is mental attitude. It might only make a difference of two or three points in the entire match, but how you play those key points often makes the difference between winning and losing. If the mind is strong, you can do almost anything you want."

I have discovered that the thinking of a confident person is what separates him or her from the crowd of people who choose to live on "Insecurity Boulevard." The confident person has developed a unique positive mental attitude that the forces of negativity can rarely penetrate. In essence, confidence is an attitude.

What is attitude? *Attitude is:*

* a positive or negative state of mind or way of thinking.
* a deep-seated, chosen belief, either positive or negative, that sets in motion corresponding behavior, generally resulting in a self-fulfilling prophecy.
* an inward feeling expressed by behavior.

Your attitude becomes a manifestation of how you think; it's a combined set of thoughts, feelings, and actions that produces a predisposition to act or react in a particular way. Your attitude is what determines your behavior or your corresponding actions. Your actions are what ultimately determine your outcomes in life. A confident, positive mental mind-set produces confident and positive actions.

Confidence can be a negative or a positive force.

Yes, confidence can become a negative force. How? You may be confident that you will not succeed or that you will not perform at your maximum potential. You can talk or think yourself into not being able to do something.

POSITIVE ATTITUDE + POSITIVE ACTIONS = POSITIVE RESULTS

Confidence can become a positive force when you combine two important elements: (1) positive attitude and (2) positive actions. Both of these elements require you to make a choice. There is a direct link between your attitude and the choices that you make. A positive attitude will respond with positive actions. You can think positively all day long but if you do not act on what you are thinking, you will not get the positive results you want.

Positive actions create successful results. However, negative attitudes produce negative actions. Negative actions produce poor results. The good news is your attitude toward life, people, and circumstances can change. Now that we have used the Inner You Triangle to look at Love, Knowledge, and

Attitude, let's return to the Attraction Triangle and the other important sides of Attraction.

Point 2—The Outer You

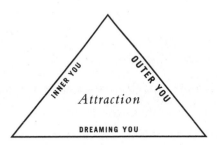

Do you remember playing in a pool or at the beach with a beach ball when you were a kid? I do. As a matter of fact, I would always try to push the beach ball down into the water and hold it as long as I could. Eventually the pressure would overwhelm me and the ball would come flying up out of the water. The same thing happens with your Inner You. Your Inner You is the ball that you can push down for a while, but it will eventually come to the surface and be seen on the outside by many.

What is going on inside you will always find expression outside of you. Your inner world will manifest your outer world.

What are some of the outward manifestations that attract people to us? Three things attract people to your Outer You: accomplishments, smile, and dress.

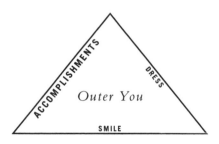

POINT 1—ACCOMPLISHMENTS

Let's face it! People are attracted to success, not failure. Nobody wants to go to the wealth seminar of Harry the Hobo. People are attracted to celebrities and experts.

Warren Buffett does not have to beg thousands of people to come to his yearly wealth conference in Omaha, Nebraska. Yes, Omaha, Nebraska. Not Hawaii, Fiji, Orlando, or Miami Beach. Yet thousands of people flock from all over the world to hear what he has to say.

I fly more than 140,000 miles a year. I hold diamond status with Delta Air Lines. I cannot tell you how many times I have sat next to somebody in first class who asked me the proverbial question "What do you do?" When I tell them I am a professional speaker, author, and America's #1 Confidence Coach, their countenance quickly changes. They normally say, "Wow, I'm sitting beside somebody famous. You're an author? That is really neat." For the next hour the person beside me will ask me one question after another about leadership, confidence, coaching, or book writing. They ask, "Do you have a card?" People want to connect with a person who has achieved something in life.

Take credit for your own achievements.

Here is an important Confidence Coaching Solution—take credit for your own achievements. I have affirmed highly "spiritual" people's success, and they say things like "It's all God!" That makes me think of the farmer who bought a barren piece of property and worked hard for years to produce crops. One day a person came by and said, "Wow, look what the Lord has done with this property!" And the man says, "You should have seen it when God had it all to himself."

You are not taking any credit away from God when you acknowledge your achievements on earth. I have complimented business owners on what a great business they have built and some have said, "I just got really lucky." They were not taking credit for their achievements. They did not just roll the dice and suddenly have a great company. They worked hard! Own the credit so your confidence can increase.

POINT 2—DRESS

Regardless of how you feel inside, always try to look like a winner.

Even if you are behind, a sustained look of control and
confidence can give you a mental edge that results in victory.

—Arthur Ashe, tennis pro

A report from Stanford University indicates that our clothes determine 55 percent of the impression we make on people. Another report claims that the right look can increase your salary by 22 percent. Seventy-five percent of U.S. workers admit that personal appearance influences attitudes and professionalism. Good hygiene, good grooming, and clean clothes are never too formal, and ripped clothes, baggy T-shirts, and wrinkled jeans are never appropriate.[11]

Those who are successful dress that way! Your personal appearance influences your confidence, attitude, and emotions. The way you look on the outside has a definite bearing on how you feel and see yourself on the inside. What you wear daily can affect you in a positive or negative way. I learned this secret several years ago.

When I woke up in the morning, I would basically dress the way I felt. If I was not in the "mood" to dress up, I would put on a pair of jeans and an old T-shirt. I noticed that throughout the day, I felt sloppy and tired, and feelings of insecurity would hit me if I received an important phone call from a client. I discovered that the sloppy clothes I put on in the

---

11 Robb Thompson, *Everyday Ways to Enjoy Success at Work* (Tinley Park, IL: RTI, 2006), p. 107.

morning gave me a sloppy feeling throughout the day. Now when I wake up feeling tired, down, or sloppy, I intentionally put on a crisp, white dress shirt and a silk tie with a nice pair of dress pants. Almost within minutes, my confidence level increases and my mood starts changing; I begin my day with a fresh surge of confidence. You will feel and become the way you decide to dress.

CONFIDENCE COACHING SOLUTION

Dress the way you want to feel, not the
way you are currently feeling.

All men are created equal, and then they get dressed.
—Advertisement for a men's clothing store

The cliché that "clothes make the man" is a half-truth. Your dress may not make you, but it surely tells a lot about you. Over 90 percent of all communication is visual, not verbal. Your personal appearance is like a billboard that tells all about you. Yes, your appearance "talks." It is saying either positive or negative things about you. When you dress for success, you present an appearance of confidence, success, wisdom, and excellence. If you dress sloppily, you present an appearance of low self-esteem, failure, ignorance, laziness, and sloppiness.

People see what we are before they hear what we say.

Therefore, your dress can influence the decisions and plans of those who see you. Your personal appearance produces an atmosphere of acceptance or rejection. As mentioned previously, you will never get a second chance to make a good first impression.

Dale Carnegie tells the story of a young man who began working as a teller at a bank. Rather than dressing like the other tellers, this man observed the wardrobe of the bank manager and dressed similarly. Soon thereafter, the bank customers, his fellow employees, his superiors, and—most important, he himself—saw him as the bank manager.

Can you guess what happened? Before long, he was promoted to that position while all the "experienced" tellers remained at their present positions.[12]

Your dress tells people where you're going in life. If you see a woman wearing a wedding gown, you know she is going to her wedding. If you see another woman wearing a bathing suit, you know she is headed for the beach. If you see a kid wearing a baseball uniform, you know he is headed to a baseball game. If you see a person wearing a clown costume, you know he is headed for the circus. If you see a man wearing a navy blue, pin-striped suit with a red tie and carrying a briefcase, you know he is going to an important business meeting. The way you are dressed tells people where you are going.

---

12 Ibid., p. 109.

POINT 3—SMILE

SMILE! Don't forget to dress your face. Use your face; it's your million-dollar asset. Many people today are spending thousands of dollars on face-lifts. There is a face-lift that you can perform on yourself that will instantly improve your facial features. You can change your appearance with a simple smile.

Do this right now—smile for about five minutes. How do you feel? Better or worse? I know that you feel better. It is almost impossible to smile on the outside and still feel insecure, doubtful, or crummy on the inside. Use your million-dollar asset as often as possible. A smile is your body's natural response when you feel happy. When you are smiling, you look and feel more confident.

Your smile always gives you an instant confidence boost. If you are not using your smile, you are like a person with a million dollars in the bank and no checkbook.

Your smile is the million-dollar asset in your human relations inventory. Contrary to our previous "seven seconds" discussion, researchers from the University of Toledo found that when people meet you for the first time, they make up their minds about your attitude within a mere fifteen seconds! Start off with a smile, and they'll remember you as a positive person forever![13]

13 "Success Secrets Super Lucky People Swear By!" *Woman's World*, April 5, 2005, p. 10.

CONFIDENCE COACHING SOLUTION

Your smile can boost somebody else's confidence.

I learned this Confidence Coaching Solution from Bonaro Overstreet. In her book *Understanding Fear in Ourselves and Others*, she writes:

> *The person at whom we smile, smiles back. In one sense, he smiles at us. In a deeper sense, his smile reports the sudden well-being we have enabled him to experience. He smiles because our smile has made him feel smile-deserving. We have, so to speak, picked him out of the crowd. We have differentiated him and given him individual status.*

What a powerful thought! A simple smile can make somebody feel important. When you make somebody feel important, you have won a friend forever. Whenever you meet somebody for the first time, smile big and that person will feel like he has known you all his life.

If you have a hard time smiling at first, don't worry about it. Go ahead and smile anyway. Say the word *cheese* to yourself in the mirror. Get your smile muscles warmed up, and you will begin to feel a surge of confidence. Remember this point: *Your actions determine your feelings just as much as your feelings determine your actions.*

Point 3—The Dreaming You

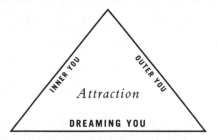

Many people think that money is the most powerful commodity on the earth . . . actually it is a dream, a vision, that unlocks attraction. Confident leaders attract others.

One of the problems I see with much of what has been written on the subject of dreams and goals is that, if we are not careful, we can start focusing so much on our own dreams and desires that we forget about reaching beyond success to significance. We focus too much on ourselves instead of making a real difference in other people's lives.

If you stop thinking about yourself and concentrate on the contribution you're making to the rest of the world, you will get more energized and will forget about your own problems and issues. This will increase your confidence and allow you to make a maximum impact, increasing your happiness and causing you to feel fulfilled. Here is the exciting thing: The more you contribute to the world around you and the dreams of others, the more you will be rewarded with abundance, personal success, significance, and recognition as a world-class leader.

Dreams keep people motivated. Dreams make a difference in our lives and the lives of others. Making a difference with dreams keeps one motivated for a lifetime. Write your dreams down. Read them to yourself out loud every day when you get up. Meditate on your dreams before you fall asleep. Let your dreams fill your day with motivation that will lift you and others up.

Exploding businesses have people who really want to be involved. Great people are attracted to them because they want to become part of an organization that is going somewhere, doing something, and make a difference in the world.

Apple's cofounder, Steve Jobs, was trying to convince John Sculley to leave his job as senior vice president of PepsiCo to become the CEO of Apple. Sculley wasn't particularly interested in leaving a secure position at Pepsi to run this brand-new company. Jobs changed Sculley's mind by asking him "Do you want to spend the rest of your life selling sugared water or do you want a chance to change the world?" Being part of a company that was doing something important is what attracted John Sculley to Apple.[14]

Focus on making a difference! Confident leaders inspire and attract quality people to help them turn dreams into reality.

---

14 Samuel R. Chand, *Ladder Shifts: New Realities, Rapid Change, Your Destiny* (Highland Park, IL: Mall Publishing Company, 2006), p. 15.

America's Confidence Coach Reminds You . . .

- The more valuable something is, the more people are drawn to it. The cheaper something is, the more invisible it becomes.
- Confident people know the importance of being seen so people will know they are attractive.
- Change your thinking from "Me" to "We." Just flip the "M."
- Nourish your potential by becoming an expert.
- Invest in your most valuable asset—you!
- Be a lifelong student. The more you learn, the more you earn, and the more self-confidence you will have.
- Preparation today gives confidence tomorrow.
- Get rid of your real handicap—a bad attitude!
- Confidence can be a negative or a positive force.
- Confident people have positive attitudes.
- Confidence will boost your paycheck.
- Dress the way you want to feel, not the way you are currently feeling.
- Dress the way you want to be addressed.
- Dressing for success improves your performance.
- Your smile can boost somebody else's confidence.

CONFIDENCE MAKEOVER STEPS NOW!

Answer these questions and take action to implement your plan.

1. What can I learn from others who are attractive? (Think of friends who have a look that you like; you may want to ask them where they buy their clothes, get their hair styled, etc.)
2. Does my appearance or image match my position? (I've known many company presidents or division heads who still dress like college students.)
3. Have you experienced some progress in position that should be reflected in your appearance and image?
4. Do I have enough energy to be attractive?
5. Am I getting the rest, exercise, and right kind of food I need to keep from feeling fatigued?
6. Do I have a future focus, dreams for the future? (I've noticed that most people whose minds are focused on the past tend to be melancholy, and those who focus on the present tend to be critical; but those who have a future focus are typically positive and attractive. Where is your focus?)

Regarding the Inner Me:

- Do I have a positive attitude?
- Am I self-centered or others-centered?
- Do I really love people?
- Do I encourage others?
- Do I ask others the right questions?

Regarding the Outer Me:

- What can I learn from others who are attractive?
- Does my appearance or image match my position?
- Do I have enough energy to be attractive?

Here are two questions that you should ask yourself each day:

- *How do I look when I go to work in the morning?*
- *What can I do to take a step up to another level in my personal appearance?*

Ask those closest to you what you can change about your appearance. Have the confidence to listen to their responses without getting offended. Put on your clothes of confidence and success today!

7. On what subject do you want to become an expert?
8. What information do you need to perform your job more confidently? (Make a list of what you need to learn and schedule a time to acquire this knowledge.)
9. Rate your attitude on a scale between 1 (negative) and 10 (positive) in the following areas:

- God   1   2   3   4   5   6   7   8   9   10

- Life   1   2   3   4   5   6   7   8   9   10

- People   1   2   3   4   5   6   7   8   9   10

- Work   1   2   3   4   5   6   7   8   9   10

- Marriage   1   2   3   4   5   6   7   8   9   10

- Money   1   2   3   4   5   6   7   8   9   10

- The world around you 1   2   3   4   5   6   7   8   9   10

10. What bad attitudes do you need to work on? (Make a list and then work on one a week.)

Chapter 10

THE CONFIDENCE TO LIVE AT YOUR PEAK

Success is peace of mind which is a direct result of self-satisfaction in knowing you made the effort to become the best of which you are capable.

—JOHN WOODEN,
coach

JOHN Wooden and his legendary UCLA dynasty won ten NCAA championships in twelve years, including winning eighty-eight straight games and having four perfect seasons. He was also named coach of the century by ESPN. In his book *Wooden on Leadership*, he writes of the key principle that he learned from his father, which he emphasized during his coaching career.

What he said about success—"winning the race"—was un-common for his time and even more uncommon today. His words are the core of my philosophy of leadership, perhaps the single most important concept I've learned and taught over the years. "Sons," he would tell my three brothers and me, "don't worry about whether you're better than somebody else, but never cease trying to be the best you can become. You have control over that; the other you don't." Time spent comparing myself to others, he cautioned, was time wasted. This is a tough lesson to learn when you're young, even tougher when you grow up. "Johnny, work hard to get as good as you can get," he'd say. "Do that and you may call yourself a success. Do less and you've fallen short." I did my best to follow Dad's advice.[1]

So, say to yourself . . . *I want to reinvent my life, explode my business, and skyrocket my income. Therefore, I must always push myself to become my personal best.* Now, I know from personal experience how very easily I can be deceived by my own exaggerated opinion of myself. I have a tendency to believe my own headlines. I often find myself thinking that I am doing my best. But I must always ask myself this self-coaching question: *Can I better my best?* The answer is always *Yes, I can better my best.* This is the true attitude for ambition that is defined as "the desire to be the best at what I do" in the dictionary. In my seminars, I often say, "I can teach you the tools for success, but you must have a personal ambition to succeed."

I want to become the best that I can be. What about you? Compete with yourself by becoming your best; then compete against yourself and compare against only yourself.

1 John Wooden, *Wooden on Leadership* (New York: McGraw-Hill, 2005), p. 6.

Focus on becoming your personal best instead of wasting your time comparing and competing.

I watched an interview with Shaquille O'Neal. When asked about being a role model for kids, he said, "I don't want to be a role model because then you are playing a role like an actor. I want to be a *real* model. I am a real person who makes mistakes, but I am working at getting better. I want people to see a *real* model and say I want to be better than Shaq." Put a picture on the wall of somebody you admire and keep saying "I'm going to be better than that person." That person becomes a Confidence Solution example to inspire you to become better than you are.

Living at Your Peak Every Day

I often travel to South Africa. One of South Africa's most famous heroes is Nelson Mandela. But depending on whom you talk to, some South Africans think he is the greatest leader in the history of the world and others think he is not even worth mentioning. However, one thing nobody can deny is his remarkable rise from being a prisoner on Robben Island to becoming the president of the entire country.

Richard Stengel, *Time* magazine editor and author of *Mandela's Way*, traveled with him almost every day for three years.

In the book's first chapter, "Courage Is Not the Absence of Fear," he reveals one of Mandela's key lessons of life: *"One had to put up a front. Sometimes it is only through putting up a brave front that you discover true courage. Sometimes the front is courage."*[2]

He concludes the chapter with this great statement:

Mandela's highest praise for someone he considered courageous is, "He did very well." By that he does not mean that the fellow was a dramatic hero or that he risked his life in a great endeavor, but that, day in and day out, he remained steady under trying circumstances. That, day in and day out, he resisted giving in to fear and anxiety. All of us are capable of that kind of bravery—and fortunately, that is the only bravery most of us are called on to demonstrate.[3]

Each new day presents us with new opportunities, challenges, problems to solve, and people to encounter. When these "life issues" present themselves, you want to be at your best. How can you always perform, speak, lead, behave, and sell (or whatever you do in life) at your best?

---

2 Richard Stengel, *Mandela's Way: Fifteen Lessons on Life, Love, and Courage* (New York: Crown Publishing Group, 2009), p. 32.

3 Ibid., pp. 34–35.

The Difference

What is the difference between winning and losing, riches and poverty, and leaders and followers? What is the difference between those who perform at their best and win, and those who perform and lose? What is the difference between those who have millions in the bank and those who do not even have a bank account because they have no money to put in it?

What is the difference between the person who was raised in the best family atmosphere but ends up with no job, and the person who is raised in poverty and in an abusive home, like I was, yet is able to travel the world, write books, and help millions of people unleash their potential?

The difference comes down to people's ability to maximize their internal and external communication that empowers them to maintain a peak confidence state and take action to produce the results they want in life.

Communication is the major force for empowering you to be at your best. Other than writing, there are two types of communication:

1. Internal—Self-talk in your mind.
2. External—Words you say out loud.

Words can move masses of people in a single direction to achieve incredible dreams. The current U.S. president, Barack

Obama, is by far one of the most gifted "large audience" communicators we have seen in the twenty-first century. He used his skill to influence Americans to vote for him in the primary election over Hillary Clinton and then over John McCain in the general election. Mandela used his communication skills to motivate the South African people to cast their votes to put him in office. More than three decades earlier, John F. Kennedy's words persuaded the American people to invest in putting a man on the moon.

How you communicate internally and externally is a tool you can use to always be at your peak, day in and day out. Just as these leaders were able to move the masses with their communication skills, so can you use your skills to move yourself toward living every day at your peak so that you will always perform at your best in every circumstance, challenge, and situation that arises.

CONFIDENCE COACHING SOLUTION

Communication can be a force to move individuals,
organizations, and nations in both positive
and negative directions.

If you are going to live life in a peak confidence state, you need to know about the Peak Performance Triangle.

Point 1—Psychology

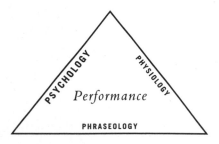

Many clients often ask me these two questions: "Why do I do what I do? Why am I having these feelings?"

In order to understand the answer to these, you must realize how your brain communicates internally. The first internal communication you need to understand is dealing with your psychology. Understanding your thinking processes as they relate to your behavior, feelings, and actions is critical for living at peak performance. This is where you learn to become your own personal psychologist.

Psychology can be defined as *the science that deals with mental processes and behavior.*

Your brain is an organ used for processing your thoughts. In an average day your mind produces more than 50,000 thoughts. Statistics show that for most people, 85 percent of these thoughts are self-doubting, negative, and self-defeating. You can condition your mind to reject all those negative thoughts and convert them into positive thoughts.

Think of it this way: Your thought factory has two bosses

in charge: Mr. Confident and Mr. Doubt, or put another way, Mr. I Can and Mr. I Can't. You can choose which boss to listen to. Which one do you listen to on a regular basis?

Living in a peak mental, emotional, and physical state is nothing more than a habit of positive thinking. Whatever you focus your thoughts on, you will feel and act accordingly. What is negative or wrong is always around you. What is positive or right is always around you. Focus on negative and wrong, and you will feel crummy, your actions will be crummy, and you will get crummy results. Focus on what's positive and right; you will feel great and get great results!

To my knowledge, medical doctors have not discovered a breakthrough confidence pill that will instantly boost your confidence. Confidence cannot be caught like a disease or physically transferred from one person to another. Confidence is a thinking process that starts in your mind. Fears, uncertainties, doubts, stresses, and feelings of depression are also emotions that have been created by your thought processes. All of these emotions start as a thinking process that you allow to flow like a river in your mind. You can make a decision about which process of thinking you are going to allow to flow in your mind.

Improve your flow—improve your life.

Confident thoughts produce the emotion of certainty that empowers a positive action and the achievement of success. (See the flow diagram on the opposite page.) Negative thinking produces negative emotions that produce negative actions and results in failure. A negative frame of mind is an energy drainer, and it takes away your confidence. Negative thinking impedes your performance, hampers your creativity, blocks your ability to think clearly, and causes you to focus on obstacles rather than opportunities.

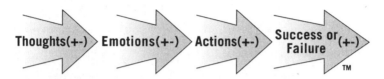

Thoughts(+-) > Emotions(+-) > Actions(+-) > Success or Failure (+-) ™

You might be asking yourself: *How can I really change the way I think, what I believe, and the way I feel about myself?* I'm glad you asked. We will walk through a three-step process that will help you reset your mind-set so you can function in your peak confidence state.

STEP 1—BUILD MENTAL TOUGHNESS

The first step toward developing mental toughness begins when you actually think about improving your mental programming. Most people never take the time to think about making adjustments in their belief systems and life. In order to improve your life for the better, you must be willing to fine-tune your thinking patterns. Living at your peak always begins in your mind. It starts with what and how you think.

World-class athletes can be physically fit, highly talented, and have home-court advantage; however, if the athletes are not mentally prepared for the game, they will not be able to perform at their maximum potential. Former football coach Bill McCartney spoke a profound truth when he said, "Mental is to physical what four is to one." No matter how smart, physically fit, or talented you may be, if you do not have a strong mental attitude, you will not succeed in life. Therefore, it is very important for you to develop a confident thought life.

The makeup of the mind includes your thoughts, beliefs, feelings, perceptions, attitudes, reflections, imaginations, intuitions, and memory. All of these aspects of your mind are affected by your memory.

Deep in your heart and mind you have stored away memories of every event in your life. Every word, book, class, song, motivational tape, television program, and every good or bad experience in life is stored somewhere in your memory banks. Each influence has had a positive or negative impact on your belief system. These influences have affected the way you think, act, speak, and even feel about yourself. Some of the bad events have had such a powerful impact on you that they continue to exercise control over your thinking years after the initial event.

No matter what you have been through or learned in the past, you can reset your mind-set and begin again. Fears, uncertainties, and doubts (FUD) are all learned feelings and behaviors. If you can learn them, you can also unlearn them. Yes, you can reprogram your mind to think like a confident champion! Don't allow restrictive belief systems to paralyze you from success another day of your life.

The most powerful muscle in changing the body is the mind.

—Quote from *Extreme Makeover* television show

The great summary statement of all religions and philosophies is this: *You become what you think about the most.* Solomon was one of the richest and wisest men in history. His insight was *"For as he thinks in his heart, so is he . . ."*[4] If you think of yourself as a loser—you are a loser. If you see yourself as a millionaire—you may become one. If you see yourself as a winner or a confident champion—you will be one. Your outer world ultimately becomes a reality of your inner world. How and what you think on the inside will become manifest on the outside.

Earl Nightingale is known as one of the world's foremost experts on success and what makes people successful. He has said, *"You become what you think about all day."*

Napoleon Hill, author of *Laws of Success, Think and Grow Rich,* and *Grow Rich with Peace of Mind,* believes that "Our brains become magnetized with the dominating thoughts which we hold in our minds, and by means with which no man is familiar, these 'magnets' attract to us the forces, the people, and the circumstances of life which harmonize with the nature of our dominating thoughts."[5]

4 Proverbs 23:7 (NKJV).

5 Napoleon Hill, *Think and Grow Rich: Your Key to Financial Wealth and Power* (New York: Tarcher, 2008), p. 9.

STEP 2—TAKE CONTROL OF YOUR EMOTIONS AND FEELINGS

I want you to take a moment to reflect. Think of a time when you did not have confidence, when you totally doubted yourself. Do you remember a time like that? What were you feeling?

Discouraged? Frustrated? Overwhelmed? Limited? Depressed? These are all descriptions of the feelings you experience when you live with self-doubt. These are probably the worst feelings you can experience in life. These feelings are a very dangerous threat to your success, happiness, and peace of mind.

Now think of a time when you felt very confident. Do you remember a time like that? What were you feeling? Did you feel especially good about yourself? Did you feel excited and full of energy?

Could you feel your adrenaline pumping? Did you feel like you could take on the world and win? These are all descriptions of the feelings you experience when confidence is present. There is truly no greater feeling than the feeling of confidence.

Let's slow down for a moment and really think about these two scenarios. What was the difference between the experience you had when you were confident and the experience you had when you were not confident? You felt confident because you were thinking confidently, right? When you felt insecure and afraid, you were self-doubting and thinking insecurely. Therefore, your thoughts or beliefs were creating

252

your feelings, whether positive or negative, depending on how you were thinking.

Is there someone you dislike, around whom you feel terrible or uncomfortable? Why do you feel that way? Because you believe that the person is bad, you have a bad feeling come over you. Your beliefs create your feeling.

STEP 3—CHANGE YOUR ACTIONS AND BEHAVIOR

Your behavior is tied to your mental and emotional states. Most people want to change, but they cannot get past their emotions or feelings. Your E-motions are what set things "IN-motion." If you do not feel confident, you will not act confidently. If you do not feel like a success in life, you will not act like a success in life. Here are six facts that you can use to change your actions by changing your thinking:

- You will have both positive and negative thoughts.
- You can control your thoughts.
- Your feelings come from your thoughts or beliefs. If your feelings are negative, check your thoughts.
- You can control your feelings by taking control of your thoughts.
- You can change your behavior by changing your feelings.
- When you change your behavior, you change your future.

If you are willing to improve your thinking processes, you can convert your negative feelings into positive feelings. When your feelings change, your actions and behaviors automatically improve for the better. Adjusting your actions and behaviors will bring positive changes to your life. Let me put it to you this way: *If you start thinking confidently, you will start feeling confident. When you start thinking and feeling confident, you will start acting confidently. When you start acting confidently, you will consistently perform at your peak performance. When you perform at your peak performance, you will enjoy the thrills of success.*

When you start thinking and feeling confident, you will look at mountains and only see anthills. You will look at obstacles and see opportunities. You will run into problems and always find solutions. Being confident will become part of your natural behavior.

When you get into this confidence flow, everything you attempt to accomplish will happen effortlessly. You will get into a perpetual flow of repetitive success. Soon, you will get to the place where you do not ever think, feel, or act like a failure.

Make a list of all the negative thoughts you have about yourself that you need to change. How will changing these thoughts change your feelings and actions?

Point 2—Physiology

Your physical body is another tool you have in your arsenal that can empower you or render you powerless to operate at your peak. This may be a new word for you so let's look at

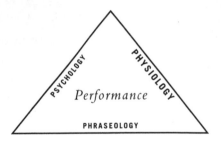

the definition. Physiology is the biological study of the functions of living organisms and their parts.

Physiology deals with how you use your physical body for things like posture, breath, smile, and movement. Both your brain and your body work in harmony together to help you operate at your peak if you know how to use them. Your physiology communicates with your brain and tells it what to do and your brain communicates to the body and tells it what to do. Almost as instantly as the mind thinks something, there is an observable response in the physical body.

I use an illustration at my meetings to emphasize the mind and body connection. I will call someone up from the audience. I ask him to hold his arm straight out to the side. I will then push down on the arm and tell him to resist me. Then I say, "Now I want us to do the same thing but I want you to remember a time in your life when you were at your peak . . . when you were doing your best. I want you to see this time in your imagination." Then I push down on his arm. I can hardly move his arm even if I use all my strength.

Then I say, "Great job! You are very strong. Now I want

you to remember the worst day of your life. Can you remember? I want you to experience all the emotion you were feeling. See the picture of that day as clear as you can." The audience will see the physiology of the person instantly change. The head drops, the shoulders slump, and the arm being held out straight starts to fall naturally. Then I take two fingers and I push the arm down with great ease.

What does this teach us? What we think affects the strength of the physical body. Our psychology affects our physiology.

I am a very animated person. Over the years I have done a lot of personal coaching and consulting with great leaders, and I have heard almost every crazy story you can think of. I have a hard time not expressing on my face what I am thinking on the inside, especially when somebody says something really off the wall. I roll my eyes or lift my eyebrows.

Your physiology communicates to people more than your words and voice tones.

Words represent 7 percent of what actually influences human behavior.

Voice qualities represent 38 percent of what influences another human being. How you use your voice will affect someone more than what you say.

Physiology represents 55 percent. The way you use your body represents the majority of what actually influences people when you communicate.[6]

6 Anthony Robbins, *Unleash the Power Within,* Seminar Notebook (San Diego: Robbins Research International, 2000), p. 11.

You can change your psychology and your emotional state by changing your physiology.

Let's do an experiment together. I want you to try an exercise for a moment. Slump your shoulders down. Now, hang your head down and add a frown on your face. Question: How do you feel?

Depressed?

Insecure?

Down on yourself?

Bad?

Sad?

One of the easiest ways to develop confidence that attracts success is to change your physical posture. Let's try another quick exercise. Hold your head up straight and look forward. Stop looking at the ground because it causes your whole body to slump over. Pull your shoulders back and stick out your chest. Add a nice smile on your face. Question: How do you feel now?

Happy?

Confident?

Proud?

Important?

Secure?

Good?

Like a champion?

Here is a powerful thing to understand about yourself. If you did the exercise, you were able to change how you felt and instantly increase your energy levels without changing the way you think or by stimulating yourself with outside sources like antidepressants, coffee, cigarettes, or drugs. You simply changed your physiology, and your emotions and feelings instantly changed.

Now, hold your head up. Straighten your shoulders. Walk with an unstoppable, confident step, as if you had somewhere important to go. Use your physiology as a tool to change your psychology, and you can instantly change how you feel.

Emotion is the product of motion. The key to success is to create patterns of movement and posture that create confidence, a sense of strength, flexibility, power, and fun. Have you ever gone on a cross-country drive that required you to be on the road late at night? I am really bad about falling asleep at the wheel, especially at night. What do you do when you start nodding off while driving? Have you ever slapped your face or just shook yourself? What happened? You experienced a quick boost of energy. You did not change your thoughts nor did you say anything. You simply changed your physiology with motion and your energy levels increased and your emotional state changed for the better.

SEVEN THINGS TO DO TO IMPROVE YOUR PHYSIOLOGY

1. Put on your million-dollar smile.

This is the quickest way to change the way you feel. It is almost impossible to smile on the outside and feel crummy on the inside. By the way, invest in your smile to make it look as nice as you can. Brush, floss, get your teeth cleaned twice a year, whiten them if they are stained from coffee or nicotine, and so on.

2. Sit up straight while sitting in a chair.

Our culture today is based on entertainment. People watch up to six hours of television a day. What is your psychology like when you watch TV? Kicked back. Relaxed. This usually means slouching in a chair. You may be doing it right now as you read this book . . . sit up in your chair right now! How do you feel?

It is said that people can only focus for thirty minutes of learning. This is true when your audience is not totally engaged. In my weekend conferences I teach students how to put themselves in a place where they can learn for *hours* at a time. If the student is totally engaged mentally and physically, there is no limit to how long he or she can learn. I guess as long as their butts can take it.

The simple act of sitting up in your seat causes your mind to be more alert and you are positioned to receive.

3. Give hugs.

Psychologist Virginia Satir has said that we need four hugs a day for survival, eight hugs a day for maintenance, and twelve hugs a day for growth.[7] Just think, by simply giving someone a hug you can make someone instantly feel better. You did not change their psychology nor did you say a word. Your physiology changes their physiology with a simple hug. By the way, hugs have been proven to improve your immune system.

4. Walk faster.

Pick up your pace. Psychologists link a poor posture and slow, sluggish walking to a negative attitude toward oneself. People who know who they are and where they are going have "pep" in their step. They naturally walk faster. People who have had a rough life and seem to be going nowhere have a shuffle in their walk. Pick up your pace, and you will feel a "pickup" in your confidence.

> *The human body is the best picture of the human soul.*
> —Ludwig Wittgenstein, philosopher

> *No citizen has a right to be an amateur in the matter of physical training . . . what a disgrace it is for a man to grow old without ever seeing the beauty and strength of which his body is capable.*
> —Socrates

7 "Virginia Satir Quotes," ThinkExist.com, http://thinkexist.com/quotation/we_need-hugs_a_day_for_survival-we_need-hugs_a/298198.html; accessed August 30, 2010.

5. Watch your body weight.

Gaining weight is something that happens to all of us. The average American gains at least one pound per year after the age of twenty-five. That means by the time you're fifty, you will have put on twenty-five pounds. In addition, your metabolism is slowing down. This causes the body to work less efficiently at burning the fat it has. At the same time, if you do not exercise, you will lose one pound of muscle per year. Losing muscle slows down your metabolism even more, and also increases the risk of injury and decreases activity performance.[8]

Don't go on a fad diet! As a matter of fact, don't go on a diet at all. Incorporate eating healthy as a lifestyle. Keep track of your calorie intake. I am amazed how thick most diet books are. My weight-loss coaching tips are really easy. Reduce the fatty foods in your diet, especially in your meat and dairy consumption. And stop eating refined sugar!

6. Exercise your way to peak performance.

Physical fitness has a huge effect on self-confidence. If you're out of shape, you'll feel insecure, unattractive, and less energetic. By working out, you improve your physical appearance, energize yourself, and accomplish something positive. Having the discipline to work out not only makes you feel better, it

---

8 Frank D. Pastorelli, *Fit for Life* (Tampa: Florida Fit Pros, 2004), pp. 16–17.

creates positive momentum that you can build on the rest of the day.

7. Drink More Water: Water = Energy.

Do you ever get really tired about three o'clock in the afternoon? I used to. So I would take a nap and then wake up fifteen minutes later feeling miserable. Or sometimes I would go to Starbucks and drink a high-octane coffee. One day somebody told me to slam down an eight-ounce glass of water when I was feeling tired and my energy levels would increase. So the next day, sure enough, around 3:00 P.M. I started feeling tired so I drank a glass of water and went back to work. The next thing I knew, I was still working at 9:00 P.M. Wow! I was sold on the idea that water equals energy. I realized I had been living in a dehydrated state.

If you suffer from inadequate hydration, you may feel tired, hungry, bloated, and sluggish.

The importance of drinking the proper amount of water cannot be stressed enough if you really want to be your best and operate at your peak every day. The body simply cannot adapt to dehydration, which impairs every psychological function of the body. Studies show that fluid loss of even two percent of body weight will adversely affect circulatory functions and decrease performance levels.[9]

9 Ibid., p. 40.

Every function, every organ, every cell in your body needs water to survive. Three out of four people today live in a dehydrated state. If 85 percent of our brains and muscles contains water, how can we possibly be performing at our best if we are dehydrated? What would happen if you sucked all the juice out of a watermelon? It would totally shrivel up. It is the same thing with the cells in your body. They need to be energized with water or they will not function at peak. But if you give your cells the fuel of water, they will respond by allowing your body to perform even better.

Point 3—Phraseology

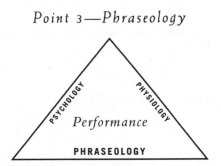

Donald Trump's phraseology is incredibly powerful. When he speaks about his new projects, he always confidently declares his properties are the biggest, most beautiful creations in the world. He has been asked about this many times. In his own words:

[The] key to the way I promote is BRAVADO. People may not always think big themselves but they get very excited by

those who do. People want to believe something is THE biggest and THE greatest and THE most spectacular. Some people have written that I'm boastful, but they are missing the point. If you're devoting your life to creating a body of work and you believe in what you do, and what you do is excellent, you'd damn well better tell people you think so. Subtlety and modesty are appropriate for nuns, but if you're in business, you'd better learn to speak up and announce your significant accomplishments to the world.[10]

Do you ever listen to people talk? If you take the time to listen to others and yourself, you will discover that people who are really confident use what I call a confidence-boosting vocabulary, and those who are lacking in confidence use what I call the loser's vocabulary.

Your daily conversations reveal whether you are a confident winner or an insecure loser. You cannot expect to reach the Winner's Circle talking like a hillbilly or a loser. Winners talk about their past and future successes and victories. Losers like to talk about all their current obstacles. Champions like to talk about possibilities. Losers talk about the impossibilities. Losers talk like victims. Winners talk like victors!

I listened to a leading neurosurgeon say that a recent medical science discovery showed that the speech center in the

---

10 Dan Kennedy, *No B.S. Wealth Attraction in the New Economy* (Irvine, CA: Entrepreneur Press, 2010), pp. 67–68.

brain exercises dominion over the whole central nervous system. He said that you can cause different parts of the body to respond by stimulating corresponding parts of the human brain, but when the speech center is stimulated, the whole central nervous system responds. Therefore, if you say things like "I am a loser" or "I am weak," the speech center sends out messages to the entire body to prepare for failure. Words birth confidence or fear, self-confidence or self-doubt, security or insecurity. Every success you experience begins with the words in your own mouth.

Just as you can use your psychology and physiology as tools to help you perform daily at your best, you can also use your phraseology—the way in which words and phrases are used in speech or writing. Phraseology is a set of expressions used by a particular person or group. We have covered your self-talk in Chapter 6. Now let's talk about your ability to verbally communicate your confidence every day.

Do you remember the old rhyme that you said as a kid, "Sticks and stones may break my bones but words will never hurt me"? Friend, nothing could be further from the truth. Words can cause wars and words can stop wars. Words can cause a divorce and words can cause a marriage to be restored. Words can and do hurt us. Especially those silent words that you speak to yourself on a daily basis—those words that nobody hears on the outside, but you hear on the inside.

Studies show that if you listen to something positive the

first twenty minutes of your day, you will increase your productivity by 37 percent.[11]

From the moment you were born, you have been conditioned with negative words. We are born to win, then almost immediately conditioned to lose. Starting in childhood, conditioning is a gradual yet consistent and relentless progression. The average fourth-grade child has heard the words "No, you can't do that" over seventy thousand times![12]

What is a "word"? This is the definition I use in my seminars: *Words are simply descriptions of pictures based on culture.*

Your phraseology combines words to communicate not only a message about what you think but also about your confidence level to others. The following are three keys to understanding the use of words in building your confidence:

KEY 1—UNDERSTAND THE POWER OF WORDS

Words are containers of power. Words have the ability to motivate you or discourage you. Words have the ability to create or destroy. Words create biochemical changes in your physical body.

Words are more powerful than thoughts.

A single word has the ability to change your psychology.

---

11 Delatorro L. McNeal, *Robbing the Grave of Its Greatness! 8 Steps to Birthing Your Best* (Tampa: Noval Idea Publishing, 2003), p. 207.

12 T. J. Hoisington, *If You Think You Can!: Thirteen Laws That Govern the Performance of High Achievers* (New York: Hoisington, 2008), p. 3.

In my seminars, I illustrate this truth by telling everybody to count to ten. When the crowd gets to about eight, I say, "Say your name." Instantly people will blurt out their name. I then say, "With three words, I was able to change your thinking process from numbers to words."

KEY 2—EVALUATE THE WAY YOU TALK

Do you carefully choose what you will say before you speak? Most people never take time to evaluate what they say or what they talk about on a daily basis. Thinking and speaking follow one another.

Your daily talk reveals your thoughts, whether it is confident thinking or the lack thereof. Not only does your daily talk reveal your thinking, it also reinforces your thinking. If you talk like a champion, you will reinforce in your mind that you are a winner. However, if you continue to talk like a loser, you will reinforce in your mind that you are meant to be a failure in life.

Do You Say Your Name with Confidence?

I believe that there is something incredibly powerful in the act of saying your name. I might even go as far as to say that it is the symbolic key to unlocking your powerful self.[13]

—Suze Orman

13 Suze Orman, *Women & Money: Owning the Power to Control Your Destiny* (New York: Spiegel & Grau, 2007), p. 245.

I meet thousands of people every year while signing books at my table at the end of every speech. I like to personalize each copy, so I ask, "What's your name?" The majority of the people will sheepishly say their name so softly I can barely hear it. Why would you say your name so quietly? Are you ashamed of your name? Are you ashamed of yourself? You shouldn't be.

In my conferences I ask everybody to introduce themselves to the person seated next to them. The noise and energy in the room increase. Then I ask the crowd, "Did you say your name in a peak-confidence manner? Did you say your name with a sense of 'I am important'"? Then I tell everybody to introduce themselves again with passion and confidence. The noise and energy in the room explode, and it takes a while to get the crowd under control again. As I sit back and watch, I can instantly see a change in everybody's physiology. They have smiles on their faces, their posture is good, and they are beaming with excitement.

Remember, if you only have seven seconds to make a great first impression, then you definitely want people to remember your name. Interestingly, the passion you add to saying your name helps embed your name in the person's subconscious mind so they will have a greater chance of recalling it.

Do you ask questions and make statements with confidence? Confident people are decisive and make statements. They know what they want and are not afraid to ask for it. Insecure people ask lots of questions, hoping people will magically know what they want. Does every statement you make sound like a question? For instance, a person wants to go to the mall shopping. So the person asks, "Are you going to the mall today?" The question is actually a hint that they want you to take them to the mall. The confident person says, "I want to go to the mall today. Can you take me?"

Do you project confident voice tones like a lion or do you sound like a pussycat?

I know a guy who is an incredibly gifted teacher and communicator. He has some great thoughts and a lot of wisdom. However, nobody wants to listen to him. Why? Because when he talks, it sounds like he is whining like a pussycat instead of talking boldly like a lion.

Are your voice tones irritating? Do your voice tones reflect a commanding confidence that causes people to want to listen to you?

Do you speak up or speak down? Insecure people tend to talk really softly and slowly. Confident people project their voice with certainty, speed, and clarity.

Do you ask negative questions and expect positive results? I was out to eat with a friend who is a coupon junkie. He had two coupons for 20 percent off and he gave one to me. When the server came to the table, my friend said, "You don't allow two coupons to be used at one table, do you?" And guess what the waiter said? "NO." Why? My friend asked with an expectation that the answer would be no.

I always expect people to do what I want them to do. I

would have said, "Please separate our two bills because we both have 20-percent-off coupons we will be using." What kind of response do you think I would get? Most likely the server would follow through.

One of my friends took me to one of his favorite restaurants. When we arrived, he said, "I hope we get good service today." Well the food was fantastic, but the service was terrible. Here is what I do when I go to a restaurant. When the server comes to the table, I say, "Sally, I heard you are one of the best servers in this restaurant. I'm sure glad I got you." Now what is Sally going to do? She is going to try to live up to her reputation of being the best, and I am going to get great service.

Ask with the confidence that people will give you what you want. Confident people are not afraid to ask for what they want. If you are denied or told no, just go on to the next question. Keep asking until you get what you want. There is a person out there, somewhere, who will give you what you want if you have the confidence to keep asking until you get it. You can get what you want! You just have to ask enough people. You may not be getting what you want because you are not asking enough people.

KEY 3—BUILD A VOCABULARY FULL OF CONFIDENT STATEMENTS

When you start changing the way you talk, you will reinforce new ways of thinking and will begin to see yourself as the confident champion you really are. When you talk like a champion, you will naturally find yourself more confident. The real key is to integrate confidence-boosting statements into your daily vocabulary. When this occurs, not only will your thinking and talking change, but, most important, your life will change.

Most people say, "Have a good day."

I say, "Create a *great day!*"

I don't want to have a good day, I want a great day. Good is the enemy of great. I don't want to just "have" a good day; I must "create" a great day if I am going to have one.

Over the past thirty years, Brian Tracy has trained more than a half-million sales professionals in twenty-three countries. In his book *Be a Sales Superstar*, he writes, "When you repeat to yourself the words 'I like myself! I'm the best! I can do it!' you boost your self-esteem and self-image to the point where eventually you feel unstoppable. You create within yourself the mind-set of a high-performance salesperson."

Confidence is the force that energizes and activates your words. However, just because you say something does not mean your words are full of confidence. Your ability to confidently communicate and talk to others is a major key to your future success.

Are you ready to activate your confidence with the Triangle of Peak Performance? Review the confidence tips on the next page and then start implementing the Confidence Solution steps!

America's Confidence Coach Reminds You . . .

- Focus on becoming your personal best instead of wasting your time comparing and competing.
- Losers think doubt and fail. Champions think confidently and win.
- Communication can be a force to move individual people, organizations, and nations in both positive and negative directions.
- Your emotions or confidence cannot become any stronger than your mental aptitude.
- Your emotions are tied to your belief system.
- To lose weight, simply think differently, eat less, and move more.
- Words can change people's lives for the better. Words can change people's lives for the worse.

CONFIDENCE MAKEOVER STEPS NOW!

Build a vocabulary of confidence. Here's how:

Remove these words:	Add these words:
I can't	I can
Impossible	Possible
Too hard	Too easy
I will try	I will do
I don't think	I know

If	I will
If only	Next time
I doubt it	I expect the best
Maybe	Positively
I don't believe	I do believe
I don't have time	I will make the time
I'm stressed	I'm motivated
I am afraid	I am confident
What if I fail	When I succeed
Yes, but	Yes, let's do it
Next week	Now!
Never	Today
I can't afford	I will find a way to pay
I wish	I want
Difficult	Challenge
I quit	I will be persistent

Write seven confident statements about yourself that you are willing to make today:

1. _____

2. _____

3. _____

4. _____

5. _____

6. _____

7. _____

Check off the steps below as you execute them today:

1. Put on your million-dollar smile.
2. Sit up straight while sitting in a chair.
3. Give hugs.
4. Walk faster.
5. Watch your body weight.
6. Exercise your way to peak performance.
7. Drink more water: Water = Energy.

Chapter 11

THE CONFIDENCE
TO PRODUCE RESULTS

∞

MY personal confidence level throughout high school was very high in the areas of sports, appearance, and social acceptance. I was the "life of the party" and the captain of my high school track team. However, my confidence level concerning my communication skills and intelligence was very poor. I did not believe I was smart. Remember, starting in kindergarten I had been told that I was stupid.

Although my parents never said these derogatory things, they never told me that I was smart either. This omission caused its own kind of damage. Toward the end of my senior year, I thought that I was not smart enough to go to college. I set a low standard for my life because of a lack of belief in myself. Instead of attending a four-year college or university like the rest of my friends, I chose to go to an auto/diesel mechanic's school because I thought it would be easier and best for me since it provided more "hands-on" training than "book" learning.

During the first week, I realized there was both book work *and* practical training. I decided to buckle down, open my books, and study. To my amazement, I discovered that I wasn't as "dumb" as I once thought. I finished the entire schooling with an A average. There was just one major problem. Although I completed the book work, I had a terrible time with the practical shop work. It became obvious that I was not designed to work with my hands. I hated working with my hands, and the thought of getting my hands greasy totally disgusted me. This is always the joke around our family gatherings today: "Keith a mechanic? Ha! He's the guy who gets pedicures and manicures."

My natural talents and abilities surfaced—networking, communicating, encouraging, and teaching others. When I was younger, I thought my time going to that technical college was wasted. However, in retrospect, I realize that it was during that time when I started believing in myself. I realized that I was intelligent. When I started believing in myself and my potential, I had the confidence needed to take action to apply to a university. Today, I have earned a master's degree and a doctoral degree from an accredited university.

This brings us to our Results Triangle: Belief + Potential + Action = Results.

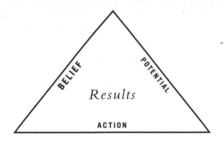

Because my belief was *I am stupid*, my *potential was crippled* and that produced an *action of not applying to a four-year college*. The result was *doing something I hated*!

Now for the good news! When my personal belief changed, my results changed.

* Belief—"I am actually smart and I can go to a regular university."
* Potential—This positive belief placed a demand on my true potential.
* Results—I earned a Ph.D.

Your personal belief systems determine how much of your potential is released in your life. How much you believe in your potential determines the force and magnitude of your actions to achieve results. The size of your actions determines the size of your results that you reap in life.

Let's look more closely at each point of the Results Triangle.

Point 1—What Are Your Beliefs?

I am convinced that 80 percent of success in life is psychology and 20 percent is mechanics. Like an onion, your internal beliefs are in layers called your belief or value systems. Your belief in the possibility of your great future determines your increasing potential. However, the layer under that belief may be even more important: *the belief in your own potential, capability, and competency.*

> *It ain't what you don't know that gets you into trouble. It's what you know for sure that just ain't so.*
>
> —Mark Twain

What is a belief? *The cognition plus emotion that creates within you the "certainty" about something.* So, it's your responsibility to identify and redirect any wrong paradigms you may have accumulated over the years.

Here is a striking but nonetheless true statistic. Did you know that almost 95 percent of your beliefs are programmed into your internal hard drive by the age of thirteen? This means the paradigms that control your life were established before you were fourteen years of age. Many of us have been programmed to be negative about ourselves and others.[1]

1 Robb Thompson, *My Total Life Makeover.* Concepts adapted from his book and CD program.

The very foundation of confidence is built on what you think, know, and ultimately believe. Beliefs are nothing more than a by-product of what you have thought about for so long that you have bought into it—always remember that. What you believe is a collection of continual thoughts that have formed themselves into a conviction or a feeling of certainty. Your personal belief in yourself, or your lack thereof, will show up in the way you talk, walk, work, and act, and the results you achieve.

Belief in yourself is the knowledge that you can do something. It is the inner feeling that makes you believe that what you undertake, you can accomplish. For the most part, all of us have the ability to look at something and know whether or not we can do it. Your beliefs control everything you do. If you believe you can or if you believe you cannot, you are correct. So, in belief there is power. Belief is positive power; disbelief is negative power.

Look at the Confidence Thermostat in Chapter 1. Notice the area that says POTENTIAL. There are three levels you can achieve based on your confidence setting: *Minimum, Mediocre, or Maximum.* Your personal belief in yourself and your future potential is like a thermostat that regulates what you can and will accomplish in life. When you change what you believe about yourself, you increase your thermostat setting and increase your potential quotient.

CONFIDENCE COACHING SOLUTION

*It is easier to believe the bad stuff about
yourself than the good stuff.*

Your mind does not have to work very hard to believe all the bad stuff you think about yourself. It is naturally easier to believe you are stupid, ugly, worthless, or a failure in life than to believe you are successful, highly talented, smart, valuable, and beautiful.

Most improvements in your life come from changing the negative beliefs or thoughts you have about yourself and your potential. Personal growth comes from changing your beliefs about what you expect you can do and about what is possible for you.

Supremely confident people think, believe, and expect with every brain cell that they will succeed and win in life. Self-doubters expect to fail or lose, or they simply do not expect success *or* failure. When you expect and believe that you *will* succeed, you will. Successful people are just ordinary people who have developed an extremely strong belief in themselves and what they can do. They have no doubts. If for some reason they do not succeed, it rarely affects their strong belief that they will succeed the next time an opportunity arises. They strongly believe in themselves and in their unique and special abilities.

You must start believing in your own personal possibilities. What do you really believe about your:

- Potential?
- Future achievements?
- Income?
- Weight?
- Relationships?

You must believe that you are smart, multitalented, gifted, good-looking, a great person, and well able to accomplish anything you set your mind to do. Believing that you can succeed makes others place confidence in you and want to follow you or at least help you achieve your dream.

The only thing that stands between a man and what he wants from life is often the will to try it and the faith to believe that it is possible.

—Richard M. DeVos, billionaire entrepreneur

UNMASKING NEGATIVE BELIEFS

You may say "I don't really have any negative belief systems." Yes, I know, I thought that way once myself so let's try this little exercise.

What is your current income? Fill in this blank. _____

Now, take the last number off the end of your income. Fill in this blank. _____

Question: Do you believe you can do some really stupid

things in one year to reduce your income to this figure? I know you answered yes just like 100 percent of our seminar participants do.

Ready for the next set of questions?

Take your current income and add another zero to the end. Fill in this blank. _____

Now here is your potential income for next year. How would you like that? As you think about this figure, I am sure you are also thinking *This is not possible.* See, you had no problem believing you could reduce your income, but you are experiencing FUD springing up all over the place when you should have the confidence by now to add the zero.

You are probably saying "Yes, but . . ."

List all your "Yes, but" statements here:

1. _____
2. _____
3. _____
4. _____
5. _____
6. _____

These are the limiting belief systems that you have embedded deeply in your mind-set.

Is this number a realistic goal? Probably not. But the point of the exercise is to reveal those hidden wrong belief systems in your subconscious.

Never protect a belief system that has not produced success, wealth, happiness, or a victory.

Do you believe you can double your income? Most people do not believe that. Okay, do you believe that in one year you can do some things that would cut your income in half? Almost everybody believes that. It is easier to believe all the bad stuff; and because we believe all the bad stuff, more bad stuff usually happens.

Money potential should never be limited to what you can afford. Did your parents, like mine, tell you repeatedly, "We cannot afford that"?

Never think or say that, and never tell your kids that. You can afford it. You might say, "But I do not have money to buy it." No problem! You just need to figure out a way to make it happen. Go to the store and buy a pack of bubble gum for $1 and teach your child to be an entrepreneur by having her sell each piece at school for 50 cents. Then she can save her money to buy whatever she wants.

I used to make the statement "They are filthy rich." Have you ever said that? It leaves the impression in your mind that anybody who got rich did it by doing something evil. Or that being classified as a "rich person" is associated with being dirty. Now that's a lie. Why don't we say "Those filthy poor people next door." We don't say that because it's insensitive.

Don't be afraid of money and getting rich. Money can fund great inventions, businesses, dreams, and projects. Money is not evil, but the *love* of money *is*. Money is not good or evil or dirty. Money is simply an enhancer. If you were a jerk without money, you become a bigger jerk with money. If you were a fantastic person without money and you get wealth, it will make you even sweeter. The best thing you can do for the poor is not be one of them. What is the real difference between the rich and the poor? I believe that the rich decided they were going to be rich and the poor never made that decision. Have you made that decision?

Extended seasons of poverty will cause you to believe things about yourself that simply are not true. My season of financial struggle almost made me begin to believe and think that I was a loser and always would be one. And some days I acted like one. When you believe things about yourself that are not true, you end up playing out the part of the negative things you believe about yourself.

Your belief about your future potential is going to shape the size of your thinking.

Where confidence is concerned, people are not measured in inches or pounds, or college degrees, or family background. They are measured by the size of their thinking. How big we think determines the size of our accomplishments.

—Source unknown

Before you can become a millionaire, you must learn to think like one.

> —Dr. Thomas Stanley, author of *The Millionaire Mind*

YOU MUST EXAMINE YOUR BELIEF SYSTEM

The significant problems we face cannot be solved at the same level of thinking we were at when we created them.

> —Albert Einstein

Crises cause your mind to be open to new information. Adopt the belief that your problems are opportunities to increase your potential. Let's turn to how potential develops.

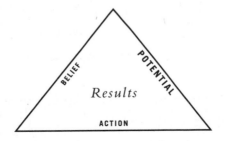

From the time you were conceived in your mother's womb, your destiny and potential started running toward your future and they are waiting for you to catch up. My definition of potential is simply the gap between your current achievements and your possibilities for the future.

What is potential? One of the most thorough definitions of potential is given by Dr. Myles Munroe. He defines your true potential this way:

POTENTIAL IS . . . unexposed ability, reserved power, untapped strength, uncapped capabilities, unused success, dormant gifts, hidden talent, and latent power.

Your Past Is Not Your Potential

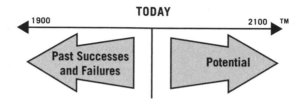

POTENTIAL IS . . . doing what you have not yet done. Going where you have not yet gone. Becoming the person you have not yet been. Imagining what you have not yet imagined. Reaching what you have not yet reached. Seeing that which you have not yet seen. Accomplishing that which you have not yet accomplished.[2]

The simple truth is that you and I have more natural potential than we could use in a lifetime. The release of your potential demands that you refuse to be satisfied with your past or latest accomplishments. What you have currently accomplished is only a fraction of what is truly possible for you.

2 Myles Munroe, *Understanding Your Potential: Discovering the Hidden You* (Shippensburg, PA: Destiny Image Publishers, 1991), introduction.

Yes, I was the best track runner on the team, but was I running at my full potential? No! My true potential had not been released yet.

Satisfaction and contentment breed unfulfilled potential.

The gap between where you are and where you want to be will always demand a new level of confidence. If you are continually stretching yourself to maximize your full potential, you should never feel satisfied, content, or comfortable. Satisfaction and contentment with your current level of success kill your potential. When you get to the place where you are content with your latest accomplishments, you put yourself into a box of containment that keeps you from accomplishing more.

Potential is crying out from your future saying, "You can be, do, have, and help more. Keep reaching."

When you perform at your best, you maximize potential. Confidence is the fuel that empowers your natural talents and causes you to perform at your maximum potential. It propels your ability to perform forward like rocket boosters send the space shuttle into orbit. Confidence is the force that launches your abilities to unlimited possibilities.

Having a high level of confidence will open doors to success, happiness, and peace of mind. However, self-doubt and insecurity will destroy or limit your natural talents, causing

you to operate far below your potential. The hidden secret to becoming more successful than you are now is to improve and strengthen the abilities, talents, and strengths you already possess by boosting your confidence.

CONFIDENCE COACHING SOLUTION

*Confidence is the power switch that empowers
you to perform at your maximum potential.*

I have read various scientific reports in the field of human potential that have estimated that we use as little as 10 percent of our abilities. This means that 90 percent of your capabilities may be lying dormant and wasted. It is sad to think that some people are only using a small portion of their abilities and talents because they lack the confidence needed to perform at their full potential. You have no idea how much talent and potential you really possess. It is time you stop allowing self-doubt and insecurity to destroy and limit your potential.

What do you think you could accomplish if you could operate at 20 percent, 40 percent, 50 percent, or even 90 percent of your abilities and talents? Without a doubt, the sky is the limit!

CONFIDENCE COACHING SOLUTION

Fear, uncertainty, and self-doubt cripple you from performing at your maximum potential.

When my confidence increased, both my performance and potential increased as well. If I had continued to listen to my self-doubts, I would have never tried to accomplish something that I had never before attempted. Thus, I would have

SELF-DOUBT
INSECURITY
FEAR

Natural
Talent

Performance
Is Below Your
Natural
Talent

™

allowed my self-doubt to cripple me from performing at my full potential. Your own perception of your potential can be a barrier to being your best. By eliminating all your self-imposed limitations, you will unlock the mighty river of potential that resides within.

CREATING RESULTS!

Dr. Thomas Stanley is the author of two best-selling books, *The Millionaire Next Door* and *The Millionaire Mind*. He has spent a great deal of his life studying the actions and thoughts of highly successful people, particularly millionaires. As mentioned in Chapter 2, Dr. Stanley conducted a national survey on the actions and thought processes used by millionaires to eliminate/reduce fears and worries when difficult circumstances arose. He received 733 responses. Here are the top ten life skills used by millionaires:

* Believing in Myself—94 percent
* Hard Work—94 percent
* Preparation—93 percent
* Focusing on Key Issues—91 percent
* Being Decisive—89 percent
* Planning—87 percent
* Being Well Organized—83 percent
* Visualizing Success—68 percent[3]

3 Thomas Stanley, *The Millionaire Mind* (Kansas City: Andrews McMeel, 2000). Report stats spread throughout book.

I was so excited when I saw this report. One thing you cannot argue with is results. Those surveyed have a proven track record—they are millionaires. Information is great, but it must be supported with results.

This survey adds fuel to my point that belief and self-confidence are the major differences between the person who lives an uncommon life and the person who lives a common life. Ninety-four percent of the millionaires surveyed indicated that a major key to their ability to overcome negativity, worry, and fear is the direct result of "believing in themselves."

I also like the fact that belief in myself and hard work were actually tied. This proves my point that believing in one's potential will cause a person to take action and work really hard. The confident person believes that he is equal to the size of his obstacles. He believes he can achieve success and significance. This man or woman will win the confidence of followers. Those who have accomplished great things in the world were not afraid of progress. They stepped out of their past prisons and into their future potential. They dared to be leaders in the midst of followers.

CONFIDENCE COACHING SOLUTION

The person who waits for safety and security never wins the big prize.

Remember, FUD are our greatest enemy.

Achievement is the crown of effort.

—James Allen, author

Some people claim that there's a woman to blame, but I know it's my own damn fault.

—Jimmy Buffett's "Margaritaville"

THE RESULTS YOU REAP DEPEND TOTALLY ON YOU!

The achievement of your dreams demands an all-out effort. It will require sacrifice and hard WORK. I know this is a dirty word in a time when everybody wants something for nothing. But I must tell you this so you will not be disappointed.

Get rid of the thought that the results you want in life lie in the hands of someone else. Instead, embrace the concept that you are the creator of your own outcomes and those results rest solely on you.

CONFIDENCE COACHING SOLUTION

The achievement of your desired result is directly proportional to the focused actions you take every day to make it happen.

The proof of desire is disciplined ACTION. Whatever you desire will only come through taking action. You will not find an achiever in history who did not pay the price of disciplined action in order to birth something of significance.

Getting results in your personal life and business will not come effortlessly. It will not happen automatically. I wish we lived in a world of genies who could blink their eyes and make things suddenly change and appear. This only happens on television, not in reality. If you want to get the results you want in life, you must put yourself on an automatic unwavering action plan.

Getting the results you want in life will not come because you are a good moral person, because you pray, because you're a spiritual person, because you're educated and smart, or because you are attractive. I know people with all these qualities who are miserable and have not achieved anything in their lives. You have to sow the seeds of disciplined action if you want to reap a perpetual harvest of abundance and achievement.

I like what Dr. Robb Thompson said in his book *The Art of Distinction*: "Procrastination is the thief of progress, robbing you of opportunity, one unproductive moment at a time."[4]

FEAR AND PROCRASTINATION:
THE TWIN THIEVES OF DISCIPLINED ACTIONS

We have already talked about how fear keeps us from taking action. Now I want to look at the second thief, which is procrastination. Procrastination. The act of procrastinating: *put-*

---

4 Robb Thompson, *The Art of Distinction: 10 Questions to Help You Separate Yourself from the Crowd* (Tinley Park, IL: RTI, 2008), p. 88.

ting off or delaying or deferring an action to a later time. It also means slowness as a consequence of not getting around to doing things.

What have you been putting off?

- *Starting a business?*
- *Firing a poor-performing employee?*
- *Improving your products?*
- *Going to college and getting a degree?*
- *Writing a book?*
- *Calling prospects?*
- *Starting to exercise?*

The 50-Percent Principle

My grandfather taught me this principle when I was trying to sell my first house. My house had been on the market for over a year with no buyers. I knew the outside of the house needed to be painted to make the home more attractive. So every time my grandfather would come over to visit me, I would start talking about my house needing to be painted. What I was really doing was throwing out a suggestion for Grandpa, since he was retired, to paint it for me. Also remember, I don't like working with my hands.

One day my grandfather said, "Keith, when you buy the

paint, the house is fifty-percent painted." I did not get the point at first, but then I realized he was teaching me that starting was 50 percent of the job. So I did what he told me, and the next day I went to the store and bought some paint and immediately called Grandpa, hoping he would offer to paint it for me. His next comment really got me; he said, "Keith, 75 percent of the job is finished as soon as you open the paint and put the brush into the paint." Wow! He was right, and three days later the house was painted and the following week we had a buyer for the home.

When you take action, doors of opportunity—*results* that have been closed—will open up for you. There is no better time to start than today. Take some sort of action toward the results you want in life. Opportunities are all around you waiting to kiss you, but opportunity is "ladylike" and you will have to take the first step to meet with her.

Have the confidence to make a committed decision to be a person who deliberately takes action. Remember, action is better than stagnation. Be guilty of taking positive actions and making a few mistakes along the way toward your desired results, but don't be found guilty of laziness and inaction.

CONFIDENCE COACHING SOLUTION

Achievers take action and can hardly be stopped.
Procrastinators never get started and allow
pebbles in the road to stop them.

Remember that Positive Belief in Yourself + Hard Work = Great Results.

The Law of Results says that if I see anybody else in this world who has achieved a result I desire, I can produce the same result if I am willing to discover how they did it, model what they did to achieve it, and pay the price of time and effort. The key is to find models of success and simply do what they have done.

MY BACKYARD FRUIT TREES

I have three fruit trees in my backyard: orange, grapefruit, and lemon. My neighbors say my trees produce the best fruit in our community. I like to compare my life to trees. The fruit on my trees represents the results I am reaping in my life. The trunk and branches represent my behavior habits and actions. And the roots represent my belief systems.

One thing I have discovered about my trees . . . the fruit never lies about the condition of the roots. If I go one year without properly watering and fertilizing my trees, my lack of attention will be revealed in both the quality and quantity of the fruit produced.

Here is my example of a tree:

- **Fruit**—*Results* Produced (achievements, potential, financial, career, weight, income, quality of friends)
- **Tree**—Behavior, Daily Habits, or Actions
- **Root**—Belief System (thoughts, values, character)

Here is one thing I have discovered: The results I am getting out of life never lie about my internal belief systems. If you don't constantly evaluate the belief systems that create your behavior, you could live your entire life reaping the fruits of negative results.

Point 3—Take Massive Action!

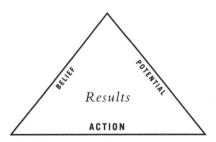

It takes guts to get out of your ruts. I call this my four-wheeling principle. When I was in college, I had a four-wheel-drive Jeep with huge tires on it for driving through very rough terrain. If you are driving on a path that has already been traveled, you can get stuck in the ruts and possibly tip over your Jeep. So sometimes I would have to do something radical to get my Jeep out of the ruts so I would not flip over. I would shift into a lower gear, press on the accelerator, and turn my steering wheel as hard as I could. Taking this radical action caused me to come out of the ruts and drive on even ground. I find a lot of leaders in organizations get stuck in ruts, and they do not know how to get out.

My job as a life and business coach is to get people, especially leaders, to take action. To break out of the ruts. Bobb Biehl gave me a great strategy to use sometimes—the Quick Results Triangle.

Explode Your Business Coaching Tip: Fire one! Hire one! Change one!

If you need to see a quick change that will produce fantastic results in your organization, do these three things:

1. Fire one unproductive problem person whom you know you should have fired a long time ago.
2. Hire one person who will help you solve your problems.
3. Make one change that everybody knows needs to be made.

Let's review our Confidence Triangle again before we move on to the final chapter.

If you have small beliefs about your potential, your potential is going to be limited and small. If your potential is small or limited, you are going to take small, if any, actions. As a result, you are going to experience a small result in your life.

Thus, the small result you reap will confirm in your mind that you were right about what you were thinking about your potential in the first place—that it is small. This flow of thinking destroys your confidence.

Now let's reverse this!

If you have outrageous beliefs about your true potential, you begin to work on maximizing your competence (talents and skills). When you maximize your competence, you are going to take *massive action* to achieve your desired result. As a result of taking such massive action, you are going reap extraordinary achievements in life. This flow of thinking will increase your confidence levels, which will enable you to live the life of your dreams.

Confidence Coaching Tips

- It is easier to believe the bad stuff about yourself than the good stuff.
- Confidence produces history changers.
- How big you think reveals your level of confidence.
- Success in life comes when you start thinking the way a king thinks.
- Your thoughts and actions are controlling where you are going in life.
- When you believe you can, your mind will design a road map to make it happen.

- Satisfaction and contentment breed unfulfilled potential.
- Confidence is the power switch that empowers you to perform at your maximum potential.
- Fear, uncertainty, and self-doubt cripple you from performing at your maximum potential.
- The person who waits for safety and security never wins the big prize.
- The achievement of your desired result is directly proportional to the focused actions you take every day to make it happen.

CONFIDENCE MAKEOVER STEPS NOW!

Not getting the results? Ask yourself these questions:

- In what area of my life am I getting negative results?
- In what area of my life do I want to get better results?
- What limiting belief systems are stopping me from getting the results I want?

Chapter 12

THE CONFIDENCE
SOLUTION FOR LIFE

∞

AFTER walking through all of the confidence coaching tips, implementing your confidence triangles, and taking your confidence steps, how important is it to you to maximize the remaining days of your life? You are now ready to move into *Life Confidence. Are you ready to step into your Confidence Solution for life? Confident people live life by design, not by default!*

Let me ask you again, *"How important is it to you to maximize the remaining days of your life?"*

If you would have asked me this question when I was sixteen, I would have replied, "I don't care about the rest of my life! I care about today! I'm going to live by my favorite song by Prince, I'm going to 'Party Like It's 1999'!"

However, the more gray hairs that appear, and the older I become, my answer to this question is now "It's very, very important to me to maximize the remaining days of my life."

Do you feel the same way? If so, I will share with you a proven process to achieve your desires and lifelong dreams.

At the age of twenty-three, I wrote down all of my lifelong dreams and goals on a yellow notepad. By the time I was thirty-eight, something great, but also tragic, happened to me: I actually achieved all of my *lifelong* dreams and goals. With the Confidence Solution, I was reinventing my life, exploding my business, and skyrocketing my income. I was implementing what I have been sharing with you throughout this book.

What do you do when you're thirty-eight and have already accomplished your goals? My dream of being married and living in a beautiful gated community had come true. My dream of having a book published and distributed in every major bookstore had come true. The dream of having a yellow Corvette convertible had become a reality. The dream of having my calendar full of scheduled speaking events and television interviews worldwide had come true. My dream of traveling the world had also come true. In the eyes of most people I had become a success.

THE MENTAL FOG

I spent the next two years of my life in a mental fog, wondering what to do with the rest of my life. I asked myself, *Where am I going? What am I going to do? What is the plan for our organization? Do I want to spend the rest of my life doing what I am doing?*

Have you ever asked yourself these types of questions about your own life, business, or organization?

I was in a state of confusion. I have always been a very focused and motivated person; however, my passion and energy
levels were dropping. I stopped writing and I spent less and less
time going to the office. I found myself just going through the
motions of my daily routine; I had lost my inner fire.

This is the mental condition I was in before I met my
mentor and now good friend, Bobb Biehl. Bobb is a consultant who has provided services for more than three thousand
high-level executives over the past thirty years. I will never
forget my first consulting session with Bobb. I explained how
I was feeling. His reply was quite life-changing for me. He
said, "Keith, you have a lot of *situational confidence*—after all,
you are an author and international speaker—but it seems as
though you lost your *Life Confidence*."

I thought to myself, *Life Confidence? What?* I had studied
the subject of confidence at least one hour a day for more than
five years. I had told thousands of people that I knew more
about confidence than anybody in the world. I had personally
read more than one hundred books on the subject, but I had
never heard anybody talk or teach about the Life Confidence
that Bobb mentioned.

After thinking for a moment, I asked Bobb, "I have never
heard of the term *Life Confidence*; will you please explain?"
Bobb said, "Life Confidence is having a crystal clear focus of
where you are going in your future and the action steps you
need to accomplish your dreams and goals. Lifelong direction
produces lifelong confidence. Keith, if you do not accomplish

anything else this year, I want you to spend the rest of this year clarifying your life purpose, dreams for the future, the goals you want to set, and a detailed action plan." The result of implementing the Confidence Solutions you have been reading in this book is LIFE CONFIDENCE.

STEP INTO YOUR FUTURE WITH LIFE CONFIDENCE!

The world makes a way for the man who knows where he is going.

—Ralph Waldo Emerson

You must see where you are going in your future before it arrives. Knowing where you are going in life produces Confidence Solutions. You are on a journey toward your destiny. You are traveling down the road to the place of sweet success. The most important thing to a traveler is direction. You must know where you are going.

I speak to more than two hundred audiences a year. I have been to some places several times. When I leave my home to go on these trips, I always leave with a sense of security and confidence because I know where I am going. I am familiar with the airports, the baggage claim areas, the rental car check-in facilities, and the directions to the hotel and to the speaking engagement facility. The moment I leave my house, I know what my day will be like, and I am confident that I will make it to my destination with ease.

However, when I have to travel to a location that I have never been to before or to a place I don't know, all kinds of insecurities start to surface. Why do these feelings surface? Because I am going somewhere I have never been before. I am not sure of my destination. I do not know where I am going.

If you do not know where you are going, how will you know when you arrive at your destination?

The very essence of leadership is that you have to have vision. You can't blow an uncertain trumpet.

—Theodore Hesburgh, president of Notre
Dame University for thirty-five years

OVERCOMING FEAR

As I have said throughout this book, I have learned that fear expresses itself in many ways. The most common fear is indecisiveness and the only solution to indecisiveness is clarity. There will always be unknowns, but indecisiveness magnifies fear and doubt. However, fear and doubt magically disappear once there is firm resolve to create a strategic plan for your future irrespective of the obstacles you are currently facing. When your destiny and dreams for the future become crystal clear, you have attained unstoppable LIFE CONFIDENCE.

WRITING YOUR PLAN

Bobb Biehl introduced me to the idea of writing out all my dreams, the needs I was going to meet, and my purpose statement with my plans, goals, successes, and ideas for the future on one piece of paper. He said, "Why would you write a huge dream on a two-by-two Post-it note? Why not have a piece of paper big enough to hold all your dreams, plans, and goals?"[1]

THE DESTINY ARROW

Why contain the plans for your destiny on a scrap of paper? Your destiny is **BIG**—your strategy should be too! The Destiny Arrow measures 22 x 36 inches. This Life Confidence exercise enables you (or a team working with you) to put your *gigantic* dream on a *gigantic* poster for all to see and run toward!

The Destiny Arrow—Hitting the Bull's-Eye

You will notice I chose an arrow hitting a target's bull's-eye. Sharpshooters will tell you that if you're going to aim for a target, you should go for the bull's-eye. That way if you miss the bull's-eye, you're still on target. But if all you do is aim for the target and you miss, you're nowhere. Don Shula, who co-authored *Everyone's a Coach* with Ken Blanchard, always told his Miami Dolphins football team that the target they were aiming at was to win every game. Was that possible? Obviously not, but if you don't shoot for excellence, you never have a chance of getting there. That's probably why

---

1 If you are serious about strategic planning, one of Bobb Biehl's books I highly recommend is *Masterplanning*. Inspired by Bobb's Masterplanning leadership program, I designed the Destiny Arrow.

Don Shula won more football games than any coach in NFL history—undefeated for an entire season. The target you aim for has a lot to do with your performance.[2]

The Destiny Arrow—The Key to Getting Things Done Faster Than You Ever Imagined

Questions worth repeating from the beginning of the book: Do you feel like you should be much further along in life by now? Do you feel like your life or business is progressing at a turtle's pace? Well, more than likely it is!

Since the beginning of time, humankind has had a passion for speed. We have taken ourselves from walking to riding horses; from the Model T to the Ford GT; from the single-engine plane to the supersonic jet to the space shuttle; from a bicycle with a small engine to a crotch-rocket motorcycle; from the oven to the microwave; mail to e-mail; and from e-mail to text messaging. We have a desire to get things done faster and quicker.

The SSC Ultimate Aero is the fastest production car in the world. SSC Ultimate Aero: 257 mph+, 0–60 in 2.7 seconds; twin-turbo V8 engine with 1,183 horsepower; base price is $654,400. This car was tested in March 2007 by Guinness World Records.

On a clear and sunny day on the autobahn, this car can reach speeds of 257 miles per hour. However, if you are driv-

2 Ken Blanchard, *Leading at a Higher Level* (Englewood Cliffs, NJ: Prentice Hall, 2007), p. 3.

A SUCCESSFUL ENTERPRISE IS BUILT BY *Wis... Pe...*

THIS IS A SAMPLE

To order THE DESTINY ARROW please call (888) 379-CONFIDENCE

Departments 4

Purpose 3

Problems 2

Destiny 1

"Begin with the end in mind."
—Stephen R. Covey

THE
CONFIDENCE
Coaching SYSTEM™

ing the SSC Ultimate Aero on a foggy day with no visibility, the speed and the rate this car reaches its final destination are quite different.

As a matter of fact, on a foggy day the Ford Focus can match the speed of the Aero because you can only drive so fast in the fog.

You can have SSC Ultimate Aero potential, but will produce a Ford Focus result if you are in the fog.

Do you remember the song "I Can See Clearly Now (the Rain Has Gone)"? Most people and business owners go through life trying to drive their life or organization in the rain and fog. They are not sure where they are going, what they want to achieve in the future, or their reason for existence.

Here are some symptoms of driving in the fog; see if they relate to your own life or organization. When you drive in the fog:

- There is hesitancy.
- Your productivity is low.
- Doubt is ever present.
- There is uncertainty.
- Your ability to make decisions is skewed.
- It produces stress.
- It produces thoughts such as *Am I ever going to get to my destination?*

It is time to get out of the fog!

The leadership process of turning a dream into reality begins with a deposit of destiny in the heart of a person to solve a major *problem* or meet an immediate *need*.

Jack Welch took over as the CEO of General Electric (GE) during a time when the company was facing some major challenges. This leader of destiny totally turned GE around. Jack stated that the first step was for the company to "define its destiny in broad but clear terms. You need an overarching message, something big, but simple and understandable."[3] What was the biggest problem General Electric was facing? Apparently the lack of a clear destiny. Jack Welch and GE came up with a statement of destiny when they set the following goal: "To become #1 or #2 in every market we serve and revolutionize this company to have the speed and agility of a small enterprise."[4]

Armed with a profoundly simple, clear, and compelling destiny, Jack Welch led GE into a new and prosperous future.

At forty-three years of age, Henry Ford wanted to improve transportation beyond the slow pace of a horse and buggy. He also wanted to meet an immediate need of producing a car that every person could afford to own. Henry Ford

3 Noel M. Tichy and Stratford Sherman, *Control Your Destiny or Someone Else Will* (New York: Doubleday Currency, 1993), pp. 245–246.

4 Robert Slater, *The New GE: How Jack Welch Revived an American Institution* (Homewood, IL: Richard D. Irwin, 1993), pp. 77–93.

led his company forward with destiny burning in his heart to "democratize the automobile." He said:

> *I will build a motor car for the great multitude . . . It will be so low in price that no man making a good salary will be unable to own one and enjoy with his family the blessing of hours of pleasure in God's great open spaces . . . everybody will be able to afford one, and everyone will have one. The horse will have disappeared from our highways, the automobile will be taken for granted.*[5]

Like Jack Welch and Henry Ford, who were ignited by a destiny that was simple, clear, and compelling, you can have a vision for a bigger and better future for your organization that will serve as a unifying focal point of productivity and achievement, and that will ultimately create immense team spirit.

You do not have to be a charismatic leader to build a great organization for the future. However, you do have to be a leader who imagines the possible and understands how to inspire and motivate others.

---

5 Henry Ford with Samuel Crowther, *My Life and Work* (Garden City, NY: Doubleday, Page & Company, 1922), p. 73; Daniel J. Boorstin, *The Americans: The Democratic Experience* (New York: Vintage Books, 1974), p. 548.

Ten Questions All Highly Confident Leaders Must Ask Themselves

Are you really serious about maximizing the rest of the days of your life? If so, you must answer ten questions:

1. *How important is it to me to maximize the rest of the days of my life?*
2. *Can I clearly explain my purpose?*
3. *Can I articulate exactly what I want to accomplish twenty years from now?*
4. *What is the very best organizational context for my dream?*
5. *What is the single best measurable indicator that I am making progress toward my dream?*
6. *If I could accomplish only three measurable priorities (goals reached, needs met, or problems solved) before I die, what would I accomplish?*
7. *What problems or needs am I uniquely qualified to solve or meet?*
8. *Do I have the right people on my team who can help me reach my dream?*
9. *Do I have a detailed strategic plan to accomplish my destiny and leave a lasting legacy?*
10. *Do I have someone in my life who is not impressed with my current accomplishments or status who will stretch me toward my full potential?*

Can you give a crystal clear answer to all of these questions? If you can't answer these questions clearly, you could be in a mental fog.

How can you know your future when you don't know enough about you?

—John Kelly, president of the International
Wealth Builders Foundation

The Destiny Arrow—Your North Star

The North Star gives clear direction and confidence to seamen. Every leader needs a stable star to look toward because confident leaders like yourself:

- *Can lose their sense of direction during an economic storm.*
- *Can lose their sense of direction after they have achieved extraordinary success.*
- *Need to avoid the drift from not having a crystal clear direction concerning the future progress of their organization.*

The Destiny Arrow Gives You Clear Direction

Have you ever known a person who didn't have a clue concerning what he or she wanted in life, yet was highly successful? I haven't. And I bet you haven't either. We all need something to aim for. The Destiny Arrow is your target, showing you what to aim at. Every leader can be classified in one of three categories:

1. No Direction = Confusion + Insecurity + No Action

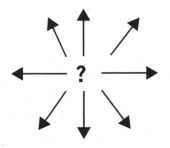

2. Unclear Direction + Action = Stress + Insecurity + Fatigue + Poor Productivity

Unclear Direction + Action =
Stress + Insecurity + Fatigue + Poor Productivity

3. Clear Direction + Action = Acceleration + Confidence + Maximum Productivity

Clear Direction + Action =
Acceleration + Confidence
+ Maximum Productivity

LIMIT THE NUMBER OF TARGETS

On the first anniversary of the creation of the citizens' group Common Cause, founder John W. Gardner wrote a summary of the rules this group had learned about influencing decision makers and accomplishing change. Included were:

- Limit the number of targets.
- Put a professional cutting edge on citizen enthusiasm.
- Form alliances.
- Tell the story.

By following these and other fundamental rules, Common Cause in its first year grew to include 250,000 members (its first-year target was only 25,000), and it continues to be an effective citizens' voice for influencing public policies.[6]

The art of turning your dreams into reality quicker and faster than you have ever imagined starts by simply getting out of the fog, becoming crystal clear about where you are going, and identifying the bull's-eye of the exact target you want to hit in the future. Ask yourself:

- *What does the picture of your future look like?*
- *How many targets are you aiming at? Have you clearly identified your company's bull's-eye? If not, why not?*

6 Bobb Biehl, *Leading with Confidence* (Peabody, MA: Aylen Publishing, 2005), p. 119.

❀ *When are you going to get serious about identifying your targets?
If not now, when?*

YOU NEED TRACTION

Stop spinning your wheels through life. Are you busy, but not going anywhere? Do you have a list of dreams and goals you want to accomplish, but nothing has happened yet? If so, you need *traction*. Your confidence needs traction!

$$TRACK + ACTION = TRACTION[7]$$

A track is a *plan*, and the Destiny Planning Arrow is a clear track for your team to follow. Some people are good at taking *action*, but they have no real plan, so they end up actively spinning their wheels. Other people are good at making plans, but they never act, so they have no *traction*. When your team has a clear TRACK and takes appropriate ACTION, you get TRACTION. When you have traction, you can accelerate your progress and productivity, which enables you, or your organization, to *achieve your destiny*.

The purpose of planning is to make you an *accomplished* person—not an active person. You can be busy all day long and not accomplish one thing. Hyperbusyness is the cocaine of the twenty-first century. People today live busier lives than

7 Inspired by Bobb Biehl, *Masterplanning* (Peabody, MA: Aylen, 2005), p. 18.

any other generation in the history of the world. Busyness, though, does not mean you are making progress or accomplishing anything. Having a strategic plan will focus your energy in one direction so you can actually be productive. Three things you must do to get traction: get clear, get focused, and get moving. Now for the Life Confidence Triangle:

The Life Confidence Triangle

Point 1—Get Clear!

Unhappiness is not knowing what we want and killing ourselves to get it.

—Don Herold, American humorist

Fundamentally, Life Confidence requires the confident leader to take responsibility for taking followers into the exciting unknown and creating a new reality for them. Where do you want your organization to be ten years from now? Do you have a written strategic plan for achieving your dreams and future goals? Without a written strategic plan, you will be tossed around by circumstances, troubles, failures, the economy, personal agendas, and possibly your own fears.

Confident leaders set clear direction for their lives. Leadership is about going somewhere. Life Confidence begins with a clear and compelling vision. A clear and compelling vision communicates specifically what type of future you want, where you want to go, why you want to go there, what needs you want to meet, what problems you want to solve, and the values you will believe in on the path to your destination.

You and the people following you in your family, organization, business, or faith community need a crystal clear picture of where you are going and why. They also need to know who is responsible for what and who is responsible for whom.

LIFE CONFIDENCE TURNS DREAMS INTO REALITY

Here is my definition of the ingredients needed in the "Life Confidence process" for turning dreams into reality and becoming a leader instead of blindly following others:

> **Leadership Process Defined:** The deposit of **destiny** in the heart of a **confident** person to solve a **problem** or meet a **need** that gives birth to a crystal clear **purpose**, organized and focused by a strategic **plan**, measured by **priorities** and goals, ignited by a **passion** that is highly **inspirational**, producing the result of **influencing PEOPLE** to get involved in making a change that benefits all of humankind.

LEADERSHIP IS A RESULT

We have just completed the Triangle of Results. An ultimate result of confidence is that you develop Life Confidence as a leader. A careful study of this definition will reveal that leadership is not a title, pursuit, method, or theory, but an end result. The end result is produced by people being influenced to help all humankind. Under this definition, the word *leader* is not a label that you give yourself. Leader is what the people whom you inspire, motivate, and ultimately influence call you because they are stirred to participate in the positive vision of the destiny that you are presenting them—whether it is the vision or destiny for a country, business, church, company, or cause. Whether the leader is Jesus Christ, Mother Teresa, Martin Luther King Jr., Nelson Mandela, or Barack Obama, they all went through this leadership process in order to influence others and make a difference in their generation and future generations.

CONFIDENT LEADERS INSPIRE THROUGH DESTINY

A further study of this definition also reveals the importance of the inspiration produced by the destiny in the heart of a leader. True leadership is influence through inspiration. If you desire to become a leader of influence and transformation, you must be able to answer these two questions: "How do I inspire others?" and "What is the *fuel* of inspiration?"

LEADERS INSPIRE THROUGH THEIR PASSION

The source of inspiration is passion—a passion that is ignited by a sense of destiny and purpose to change the world that is beyond the borders of self and personal gain. Leadership passion is birthed from a destiny and purpose that is not just something to live for, but also to die for.

How do you inspire? A leader with Life Confidence inspires by communicating a crystal clear destiny, purpose, and strategic plan for the future. Destiny and purpose should unlock a leader's passion. Leaders are able to effectively express their inner passions, which find a common purpose in the hearts of others. It is passion in the heart of the leader that attracts the people they need to help them take action to achieve the desired results.

THE ATTRACTION FACTOR

Confident leaders focus on the organization's leadership process, not its packaging, to attract new people. Growing organizations have people who really want to be involved. It's not the product or service you are providing, the stock options, the fringe benefits, or the salary that attracts great people. Great people are attracted because they want to become part of an organization that is going somewhere, that is doing something, that is changing the world.

Point 2—Get Focused!

Leadership is the capacity to translate vision into reality.

—Warren Bennis, American scholar

Confident leaders are focused on the future. They work from the future back to the present to show others how to achieve their vision. Managers conceptualize by working from the past to get to the present. They build on the past to work efficiently in the present. Managers tend to simply do what they are told and do not challenge the status quo, former policies, or old and outdated methods. Leaders know the price of progress is change and innovation.

The majority of people in the world think, work, and plan from a manager's perspective instead of a confident leader's perspective. This is the reason why most people try to start planning from where they are to where they want to go. However, I believe Stephen Covey was right when he said we should "begin with the end in mind." You will notice this quote is positioned on your Destiny Arrow just above the target.

THE POWER OF FOCUS

I never hit a shot, not even in practice, without having a very sharp, in-focus picture of it in my head. First I see the ball where I want it to finish, nice and white and sitting up high on the bright green grass. Then the scene quickly changes, and I see the ball going there: its path, trajectory, and shape, even its behavior on landing. Then there is a sort of fade-out, and the next scene shows me making the kind of swing that will turn the previous images into reality.[8]

—Jack Nicklaus

Phenomenal success is the natural outcome of focused Life Confidence. Companies invest $2.4 million for one commercial during the Super Bowl to capture one minute of your concentrated focus. The main reason most people struggle professionally and personally is simply lack of focus. They allow themselves to be easily distracted and interrupted.

Every great life has a focus. Focus equals power. Focus gives you both strength and direction. A majority of leaders can do twenty different things at once and do them all well. Most leaders today are living scattered, frantic lives that desperately need a focus. Day by day they add more and more activities but are not seeing progress. The missing piece of the puzzle is their lack of focus. When you start understanding

8 Jack Canfield, *The Success Principles: How to Get From Where You Are to Where You Want to Be* (New York: Harper Paperbacks, 2006), p. 473.

and applying the principle of focus to your life or organization, you will become a virtually unstoppable force.

Lion trainers take a stool into the cage with them. Why a stool? It tames the lion better than anything. When the trainer holds the stool with the legs extended toward the lion's face, the animal tries to focus on all four legs at once, which paralyzes him. Divided focus will do the same thing to you; it will paralyze your forward progress. Divided focus always works against you.

Why focus your life or organization? You want to go through the focusing process because it will move you in a specific direction to become something, to accomplish a dream, to make a significant difference, and to maximize your life and organization. It is important to focus your life and/or organization so you will avoid the pain of confusion, inaction, and burnout.[9]

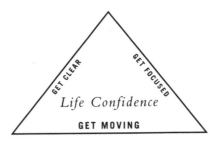

9 An online resource for you: Focusing Your Life Questions—Ten questions every successful leader must ask himself or herself in order to stay focused on daily, weekly, monthly, and yearly priorities. Visit www.LeadersofDestiny.com to download this resource.

Many people think that strategic planning is a drag so they procrastinate and never move to design a plan for the future. Creating a strategic plan can actually be exciting and energizing when done together as a team.

To get motivated toward creating strategic plans for the future, ask yourself this question: *What has my lack of clear direction cost me and my organization in the past?*

Doing means overcoming procrastination!

No, not someday . . . today! No question, the key to long-term success is constantly taking positive action to move in the direction of your dreams and goals for the future. It is time to get moving! Start preparing your strategic plan now.

Your destiny can only be reached with Life Confidence through the vehicle of a proven strategic plan in which you must fervently believe and upon which you must vigorously act. There is no other route to outrageous success.

THE ART OF STRATEGIC PLANNING

Every successful leader I've ever known has possessed passion and vision. But not every person with passion and vision becomes a successful leader. What makes the difference? Leadership! That's why I say that everything rises and falls on leadership.

—Dr. John Maxwell

Some people say that desperate times demand desperate actions. I disagree. I say that desperate times demand *strategic planning.*

Leaders of destiny understand the importance of turning their vision into a strategic plan. Many people have great dreams, goals, and desires for a better tomorrow. However, many of these dreams, goals, and desires will never come to pass unless you develop a strategic plan and then work the plan. Your destiny tells you *where* you want to go, your dreams and goals tell you *when* you want to get there, and a strategic plan tells you *how* you are going to do it. As a leader, you must turn your destiny, dreams, and goals into a written strategic plan.

Leaders of destiny know that hoping and wishing are not a strategy. They know that a vision without a strategic plan is only a fantasy, and that they cannot be strategic if their efforts lack context.

A fool with a plan can outsmart a genius with no plan.
—T. Boone Pickens, Texas billionaire and
successful businessman

Surprisingly, I have found that very few businesses, colleges, nonprofit organizations, television stations, and churches have detailed written plans for their futures. Many organizations have a one-year plan or a one-year budget, but few have a detailed ten- to twenty-year plan. In my own personal observations, only about 5 percent of companies and organizations have such a plan. The 5 percent that do have a strategic plan are also listed as the top 5 percent in their field. Interestingly, I have found that 95 percent of all project failures are the result of improper planning.

Why don't more people and organizations plan for the future? Because planning is not easy. If planning were easy, everybody would be doing it based on the results it produces. I don't like planning myself. However, I discovered that planning can be easy if I have the right tools to help me in the process. The Destiny Arrow is a tool designed to help you make the planning process easy, quick, and fun.

LIVE YOUR LIFE BY DESIGN, NOT BY DEFAULT— HAVE A STRATEGIC PLAN

Make no little plans. There is nothing in little plans to stir men's blood. Make big plans. Once a big idea is recorded, it can never die.

—Daniel Burnham, Chicago Planning Commission

What is a plan? The definition of *planning* is:

- To think out a way to do something.
- To come up with a creative way of causing something to come to pass.

- A detailed method, thought out beforehand.
- To design something that emphasizes the outcome.

With Life Confidence, you must think ahead. To create a plan, you have to think ahead. Those who think ahead—get ahead! You would not consider building a house without a blueprint. Why would you start your life or business without a plan? Sadly, most people spend more time planning their vacations than they do their lives.

Studies show that ten minutes of planning create an additional four hours of productivity in your day.[10] Organize your life. Plan your daily activities. What are you going to do every day to achieve your dreams and goals? Plan the use of your time; don't just react to circumstances. Use a calendar and make a daily list of things you need to accomplish. If you don't control your time, everything or everybody else will control you.

When you do not have a clear picture of where you are going, a certain level of uncertainty arises. Writing down your personal dreams, goals, and plans for the future gives you a clear picture of where you want to go. When you have a clear picture of where you want to go, you step into your future with confidence.

---

10 Adapted from Keith Johnson, *The Confidence Makeover* (Spring Hill, FL: Keith Johnson International, 2006).

DON'T JUST THINK IT, INK IT!

Committing your goals to paper increases the likelihood of you achieving them one thousand percent!

—Brian Tracy

John Maxwell said, "A masterfully written plan is confidence on paper. If your plan is as strong as it should be, your charming personality will be the icing on the cake. Without a written plan, you may be wearing the cake!"[11] Don't just think it, ink it! Put your confidence on paper. It is not enough for you to have a forceful and charismatic personality. Your ability to sway the masses will only work in the short term and will not accomplish massive undertakings.

Effective leadership begins with a crystal clear and compelling vision. Your first responsibility as a leader is to see—if you can't see the future, you can't lead others into it. If you do not have a vision for the future, you do not have a future. You can have a life without a vision, but you do not have a future without a vision.

Mature leaders put process between a decision that needs to be made and the time frame in which the decision is actually made. Immature leaders make decisions instantly without the process of thinking through the different options, looking

11 Ibid. p. 230.

over objectives and priorities for the year, or obtaining feedback from wise counsel.

The foundational building block for making wise decisions is a strategic plan. It takes time to go through the planning process and most immature leaders do not want to take the time to go through the process. Over the years, I have seen leaders make some very unwise short-term decisions that literally caused the downfall of entire organizations because they did not have any long-term plans. When you have clear long-term plans, immediate decision making is easier. Wise decisions are rarely made when you do not have a road map to where you are going.

The best time to start developing a strategic plan is when you are embarking on a new business or project, when you are preparing for future changes, or when you just need to clarify your plans for the future.

DEFINING STRATEGIC PLANNING

What is strategic planning? It is simply writing a statement that communicates to yourself and a group of people the direction, organizational structure, and the resources available to accomplish a dream.

Strategic planning:

- Provides a unified set of plans for all levels of leadership
- Is the foundation for creating a healthy team environment
- Provides a shared basis for clear decision making

- Is a platform for problem solving
- Provides a clear way to tell others "who we are"
- Is a system to allow fast growth
- Increases your leadership and Life Confidence

A person or a company that does not have a strategic plan is likely to suffer these painful results:

- Unclear direction
- Foggy communication
- Hidden personal agendas
- Political games
- Interdepartmental rivalry
- Frustration from staff who wonder who is responsible for what, who's responsible for whom, how much is available for what, etc.
- Procrastination in decision making
- Wasted energy and resources
- Wasted time
- Slow productivity
- Poor quality of service
- Foggy about the future
- No preparation for growth
- Chaos

Strategic planning is like harnessing twelve wild and powerful horses to a single plow; it coordinates all the energy, power, and potential to a single task, and moves in a single direction.

ARE YOUR TIRES ALIGNED?

The Destiny Planning Arrow helps you get your organization aligned. Suppose one of your car's front tires was out of alignment. How would this one tire affect the handling performance of your car? The car would pull to the left or the right, causing all the other wheels to perform below their maximum potential. The one out-of-line tire will affect the performance and outcome of the rest of the car. This is what happens when the vision of the leader is different from the vision of the people.

The Destiny Arrow helps you get all your wheels, people, or departments in alignment with your destiny and purpose for existence, empowering you or your organization to operate at peak performance.

Please don't be deceived; the tire that is out of alignment will not correct itself! Changes must be intentionally made. Many leaders tend to ignore problem people and poor-performing departments that are out of alignment and hope, wish, and pray that things will just "work out in time." Over the past fifteen years of helping leaders, I have found that the tire actually gets worse over time and so does the performance of departments that are out of alignment. I am sure you have found that when one department is out of alignment, the rest of the organization is affected.

A Leader with Life Confidence Asks This Power Question:

Do you have the right people on your team to take you to the next level and beyond?

Unleash Possibilities!

In a twenty-year period you can accomplish almost anything you desire. Just consider: Once U.S. leaders made up their minds to put a man on the moon, it took only eight years to accomplish the goal. Bill Gates, America's richest man in 1995, was nearly penniless in 1975. How were these feats accomplished? There were leaders with Life Confidence who deliberately refused to look at their present condition and started dreaming and planning for a great new future.

With Your Newly Developed Life Confidence, Use Your Destiny Planning Arrow Now!

The Destiny Planning Arrow is a tool that lasts a lifetime. No matter what you have to plan, engaging the Destiny Arrow will help clarify your basic direction. After you complete your Strategic Planning Arrow, you never have to start over! If you ever feel out of focus, reviewing your plan will give you a renewed, clear perspective.

"Just Do It" and step into Life Confidence!

FINAL WORD

∞

Our greatest fear is not that we are inadequate. Our deepest fear is that we are powerful beyond measure. It is our light, not our darkness, that most frightens us. We ask ourselves, who am I to be brilliant, gorgeous, talented, and fabulous? Actually, who are you not to be? YOU ARE A CHILD OF GOD. Your playing small doesn't serve the world. There's nothing enlightened about shrinking so that other people won't feel insecure around you. . . . We are born to manifest the Glory of God that is within us. It's not just in some of us. It's in everyone. And as we let our own light shine, we unconsciously give others permission to do the same. As we are liberated from our own fear, our presence automatically liberates others.

—MARIANNE WILLIAMSON

It is in your moment of decision that your destiny is shaped.

—ANTHONY ROBBINS

Confident People Are Not Afraid
to Make Decisions

The ability to make a decision is what separates followers from leaders, winners from losers, the rich from the poor, and the confident from the insecure.

Life is full of decisions. What clothes will I wear? What college should I attend? Should I go to college at all? What church should I attend? Which job should I take? What stocks should I invest in? What kind of business should I start? Where should I start my business? What contractor am I going to use? Where am I going to live? The questions are endless.

We are on a journey filled with questions. Where do I go next? What do I do now? How am I going to get there? A degree of uncertainty is a natural part of life and a natural part of decision making. However, decisions have to be made. Clear decisions. If you are going to wait around until there is certainty about what you should do, you will be talking about the decision until you are one hundred years old.

For every success story there must be a confident decision to do what is necessary to arrive there. On the other hand, for every failure or tragedy there is a lack of decision to execute what the leaders knew would work. Decisions create present and future events.

There are only two types of decisions: right and wrong.

Your success in life depends on making the right choices. If you make a right decision in your life, you may never know it. However, if you make a wrong decision, I guarantee you will know it.

When making a decision, you must ask yourself this important question: "Is the timing right?"

The wrong decision at the wrong time = Disaster
The wrong decision at the right time = Mistake
The right decision at the wrong time = Unacceptance
The right decision at the right time = Success[1]

Decision is . . . the act of reaching a conclusion.
Decision is . . . to make up one's mind.
Decision is . . . information acted upon.
Decision is . . . a no-turning-back commitment.

Many people govern their lives around indecision. A person who hesitates can miss great opportunities. Confidence will cause you to jump at opportunities that come your way. I can trace every mistake I made in my life to a bad decision or to no decision at all.

Life is shaped in the moment of decision, so make the right decisions.

1 John C. Maxwell, *Developing the Leader Within You* (Nashville: Thomas Nelson, 2000), p. 63.

❧ *Make a decision to get better.*

❧ *Make a decision to get richer.*

❧ *Make a decision to improve your performance.*

❧ *Make a decision to reinvent yourself.*

❧ *Make a decision to become who you really are.*

❧ *Make a decision to better your best.*

❧ *Make a decision to be happy.*

❧ *Make a decision to be healthy.*

❧ *Make a decision to be wealthy.*

❧ *Make a decision to keep moving forward.*

❧ *Make a decision to be confident.*

❧ *Make a decision to reinvent yourself, explode your business, and skyrocket your income!*

❧ *Make a decision to create a detailed strategic plan for your Confidence Solution!*

Kay, an overweight, depressed, purposeless single woman, needed to reinvent her life. At 325 pounds, she was still living with her parents although she was in her late twenties. She went through my 30-Day Confidence Coaching system and kept reading my materials over and over again. Her self-image started to change, and she decided to create a strategic plan for her Confidence Solution. As she implemented her plan, she lost more than 150 pounds.

She contacted me and I coached her in discovering her purpose; she discovered a passion for firefighters and their mission of public service. Seeing the need to improve local fire service, she decided to run for office. Pounding the pavement, shaking hands, passing out campaign literature, and attending scores of public meetings, she campaigned herself into victory, a county commission seat, and a reinvented life. Her Confidence Solution worked!

Another mentee of mine was living in a mental institution. As a result of my coaching, he strategized a Confidence Solution to get a government job and become involved in local politics. His income and confidence skyrocketed. As a result of implementing a Confidence Solution strategy and my coaching him, he now earns a six-figure income and has prominence and influence in the community.

Another client had a business stuck at $4 million gross revenue for years. He, his wife, and all his employees went through a Confidence Solution strategy to explode the business. He also brought all of his sales team to my "Selling With Confidence" seminar. In two years he doubled his gross cash flow and increased his profit margins by more than 8 percent. He also went through my Destiny Arrow strategy program and laid out a plan to grow the business long-term. This Confidence Solution for himself, his family, and his employees not only grew his business, it also gave him more free time from the business to enjoy life with his family.

What's the common denominator among these three reinvented, confident leaders?

Confidence. *Making a decision* to develop a well-planned, detailed *strategy* involving my materials, coaching, and assistance in reinventing their lives, exploding their businesses, and skyrocketing their income.

What do you need . . .

- To go through each Confidence Coaching Solution again for yourself?
- To retrace your steps at the end of each chapter?
- To go to www.KeithJohnson.TV and decide for yourself to work with me in developing your detailed strategy for success?
- Attend one of our live confidence-building seminars.

The decision is yours. Don't procrastinate!

Implement your Confidence Solution and your strategy for reinventing yourself, exploding your business, and skyrocketing your income now!

Let's Get Connected!

To request Keith Johnson to speak at your next event or for personal or business coaching, contact:

www.DrKeithJohnson.com
Connect@KeithJohnson.TV
1-888-379-Confidence (2663)
Twitter.com/drkeithjohnson
Facebook.com/drkeithjohnson
LinkedIn.com/in/drkeithjohnson

Unleash your inner winner

with these first-class titles from the

TARCHER MASTER MIND EDITIONS

THE NOW HABIT
ISBN 978-1-58542-552-5

Over 75,000 copies sold

Whether you are a professional, a student, or a homemaker, Neil Fiore, Ph.D., will help you achieve your goals more rapidly—be they large, complex challenges or the small but essential tasks of everyday life and work. The techniques in *The Now Habit* will help all busy people achieve their goals skillfully, and eliminate the anxiety and stress brought on by the workplace's pressing deadlines.

THE PROSPERITY PLAN
ISBN 978-1-58542-856-4

The rules have changed. The old strategies of hard work, fitting in, and loyalty no longer guarantee a secure and shiny future. In *The Prosperity Plan*, Laura B. Fortgang offers a simple and clear approach to building financial and emotional security. This simple ten-step guide will show you how to beat the odds and prosper in ways you never dreamed possible!

Unleash your inner winner
with these first-class titles from the

TARCHER MASTER MIND EDITIONS

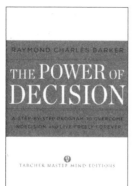

THE POWER OF DECISION
ISBN 978-1-58542-854-0

Every great achievement the world has ever seen was born with a single thought. Every great person who ever lived has been a person of decision. Raymond Charles Barker's *The Power of Decision* reveals these principles of success, and illustrates the conscious-minded choices that all of us are capable of making in order to transform our lives and make our dreams come true.

THE CONFIDENCE SOLUTION
ISBN 978-1-58542-865-6

With a blend of his trademark humor, insight, and experience, America's #1 Confidence Coach, Dr. Keith Johnson, shows how all people can achieve their dreams and desires, and realize their full potential. Finally, recognize your inner strengths and talents, boost your confidence, and become a more successful person.